NEW YORK FASHION WEEK

THE DESIGNERS, THE MODELS, THE FASHIONS OF THE BRYANT PARK ERA

EILA MELL

Photography by Randy Brooke and Roxanne Lowit

Running Press
PHILADELPHIA • LONDON

Designed by Amanda Richmond
Edited by Cindy De La Hoz
Typography: Bodoni and Neutra

Running Press Book Publishers
2300 Chestnut Street
Philadelphia, PA 19103-4371

Visit us on the web!
www.runningpress.com

TABLE OF CONTENTS

5 FOREWORD

7 IN THE BEGINNING

8 SPRING/SUMMER 1994
The First Season

18 FALL/WINTER 1994
A Colorful Season

28 SPRING/SUMMER 1995
A Ladylike Season

40 FALL/WINTER 1995
A Dark Season

50 SPRING/SUMMER 1996
The European Invasion

58 FALL/WINTER 1996
A Softer Season

70 SPRING/SUMMER 1997
Celebrating the Feminine Form

80 FALL/WINTER 1997
A Tailored Season

92 SPRING/SUMMER 1998
A Change of Venue

100 FALL/WINTER 1998
*Running in Heels . . .
Back to Bryant Park*

110 SPRING/SUMMER 1999
Changing the Fashion Calendar

120 FALL/WINTER 1999
Getting Ready for the Year 2000

130 SPRING/SUMMER 2000
Denim Everywhere

140 FALL/WINTER 2000
A Luxurious Season

150 SPRING/SUMMER 2001
Waist Management

158 FALL/WINTER 2001
Propriety and a Runaway Goat

169 SEPTEMBER 11, 2001

170 FALL/WINTER 2002
A Return to the Tents

180 SPRING/SUMMER 2003
A Pretty Season

190 FALL/WINTER 2003
A Mod Season

202 SPRING/SUMMER 2004
Vacation Mode

212 FALL/WINTER 2004
A Feminine Season

224 SPRING/SUMMER 2005
A Classic Season

234 FALL/WINTER 2005
Serious Fashion

246 SPRING/SUMMER 2006
A Romantic Season

256 FALL/WINTER 2006
A Season of Black

266 SPRING/SUMMER 2007
A Looser Season

278 FALL/WINTER 2007
A Gray Season

289 SPRING/SUMMER 2008
A Sexy Season

298 FALL/WINTER 2008
Anything Goes

308 SPRING/SUMMER 2009
Recession Fashion

316 FALL/WINTER 2009
An Exotic Season

328 SPRING/SUMMER 2010
A Sporty Season

340 FALL/WINTER 2010
Mad Men Mania

350 SPRING/SUMMER 2011
A New Home

363 INDEX

368 PHOTOGRAPHY CREDITS/
ACKNOWLEDGMENTS

FOREWORD

BY PHILLIP BLOCH

WHEN I WAS JUST A LITTLE FASH-
ionista in the 'hood I asked my mother,
"What will I be? Will I be handsome?
Will I be rich?" Here's what she said to me: "Que
sera sera, whatever will be will be. The future's not
ours to see . . . Que sera!"

Even in my wildest dreams I couldn't have dreamt
how amazing my fashionable life and career would be
as I anxiously awaited each month to make my pil-
grimage to the corner store for the arrival of the
newest magazines. My local 7-11 store was a mecca
for style, fashion, glamour, and all things that were
beyond my sequestered little world in Long Island,
New York. As a fashion over-achiever, I devoured
anything that spoke to my passion for fashion and the
fabulous life. I wanted to know what my favorite
icons like Cher, Liz Taylor, Raquel Welch, Elizabeth
Montgomery, and David Cassidy were doing or wearing. I had always imagined that my *real* mother was
Sophia Loren and she had given me up for adoption
at birth and that's how I ended up feeling so out of
place with my uncool mom and so unstylish father in
our humble home. There could be no other excuse for
this intense longing I felt for places like New York
City, where lights sparkle and dreams come true.

Though my parents loved me, understanding me
wasn't easy, but they always encouraged me to be me.
So much so, that as I was about to be expelled for the
umpteenth time, my parents met with my teachers
and begged for help to get me on a positive course.
Soon after I saw the movie *Mahogany* and it became
abundantly clear that the 9-to-5 and picket fence
would never be enough for this future renaissance
man. When I left the theater after the movie, I knew
my calling would be to become a supermodel and
fashion designer. I would be photographed at the
most exotic places with the most fascinating and creative people. I would write and be written about—
just like my heroine, Diana Ross, in *Mahogany*!

With concern and patience, the faculty at school and
my folks created a curriculum, designed with my
fashion acuity in mind (How chic! My classes were
designed for me—just like couture!), with a mini-
mum of math and science and a maximum of art and
costume history, advertising and design, sketching
and painting. Destiny had called and fashion and art
were my tickets to a brighter, more luxurious future
of dreams coming true!

When I received my advance copy (another perk of
being fabulous!) of Eila Mell's *New York Fashion
Week*, I remembered those simple days in Long
Island and realized that had I a guide like this, I may
not have felt so out of place in my own place. This
book is a treasure trove of all things fashion, jam-
packed with tantalizing trivia and information about
the early days of 7th on 6th Fashion Week at Bryant
Park.

It reads like a fashion bible, with the gospel of
trends and insider factoids that every fashionista,
young and old, will take in with insatiable delight.
This book will make even novices feel as if they're
sitting front row, center. Eila takes us through the ups
and downs of hemlines and waistlines, the ins and
outs of models' careers, designers' dreams, and New
York's finest fashion houses. This all-encompassing
read gives an inside look at all the glitz and glamour,
blood, sweat, tears, and trends that make fashion
shows and fashion such a magical and mystical ride.

Eila shares a seamlessly stitched together and in-
depth retrospective of the thoughts and journeys of
some of the most interesting and intriguing characters behind the seams, on the runways, and in front of
the camera that make the fashion business a lifestyle
beyond this little boy's most magical dreams.
Whether you were there or just wish you had been,
New York Fashion Week is a romantic diary and intimate view of a fashionable world that I will always
love to love.

IN THE BEGINNING

IN 1943, AMERICAN FASHION publicist Eleanor Lambert organized an event called Press Week. Lambert wanted to call fashion editors' attention to American designers, who had typically been overshadowed by their European counterparts. In the 1940s the shows were held at the Plaza and Pierre hotels in New York. Not long after, leading fashion publications *Vogue* and *Harper's Bazaar* began to incorporate the work of those American designers in their pages. Press Week was a success and became a tradition that continues to this day, although it is now called Fashion Week.

Over time, designers branched out from the usual Press Week locations, with many opting to present their collections in their own showrooms. It was also common to have fashion shows in nightclubs, restaurants, and other unique locations around the city. There could be fifty different shows in fifty different locations. While this worked for designers, it was inconvenient for editors and retailers as it drastically limited the number of shows one could attend. In addition, the unique venues selected by designers were often overcrowded and ill-equipped to accommodate a large audience. Attendees had to contend with situations such as power outages that left the crowd in the dark save for the faint illumination provided by cigarette lighters.

In 1991, Fern Mallis became the Executive Director of the Council of Fashion Designers of America, or CFDA (created by Eleanor Lambert). She was well aware that the situation with the shows had gotten out of hand. The final straw happened at a Michael Kors show: "He had all the famous supermodels walking—Cindy, Linda, Naomi, Claudia," said Mallis. "It was in a loft space where he had a showroom, but it was on an empty floor. It was all concrete, and filled with cheap folding chairs. When they turned the music on, the bass was so loud that everything started to shake and the ceiling started to crumble. It brushed the shoul-

ders of the models as they walked. True to form, they kept right on walking, but pieces of plaster and chunks of the ceiling landed on people's laps.

"Two of those hit with plaster were fashion journalists Suzy Menkes and Carrie Donovan. Suzy and Carrie were the poster girls for what happened, and wrote the next day, 'We live for fashion. We don't want to die for it.' It became very clear to me then and there that my job description had just changed. It became a mission to organize and centralize, to do something safe. It was also my mission as director of CFDA to look at ways to elevate the American fashion industry and create a platform to promote and talk about what the designers do. Fashion Week became my platform."

With the support of then CFDA president Stan Herman, Fern Mallis started reaching out to others with the idea. She met with resistance from some of the designers who felt that the location of their show was what it was all about, and didn't want to present their work where other designers were showing. "It was not easy to demonstrate to them how important this was," said Mallis. "In 1992 the Democratic party nominated Bill Clinton to be its candidate. As the director of the CFDA, I sat on a year-long table with all the other leaders of different industries—the theater, museums, hospitals, travel, entertainment—who would all meet as a host committee to figure out what to do for the delegates and the press when they were in town for the convention. The fashion industry decided to put on a show for them.

"We had Sheep Meadow in Central Park. We put up a tent and had about twelve hundred people there and had every designer participate. Every one of them walked down the runway at the end of the show with their model. Anna Sui was there—Donna Karan, Diane von Furstenberg, Calvin Klein, Ralph Lauren, Oscar de la Renta, Bill Blass, Isaac Mizrahi, Todd Oldham, Betsey Johnson, Tommy Hilfiger, Mary McFadden, you name it. They were all there. They all came because it was a big deal to be in this show. Afterwards, we were all on the lawn looking at this tent. It was very clear and everybody said, 'Is this what you're talking about? Is this what you want to do?' And I said, 'Exactly. This is it. Now you get it.' They saw the staging area and backstage. Everybody could see from all the seats. It was better than all the little showrooms where people were being crammed in like crazy, and empty lofts where columns were in everybody's way. This was really marvelous."

After trips to Paris and Milan to see how their shows were organized, Mallis had a meeting with three of the foremost designers of the day—Donna Karan, Calvin Klein, and Ralph Lauren. She told them they would be crazy to continue showing the way they had been: "The rooms were fire traps. The fire department would shut them down if they knew the show was going on because there wasn't any emergency exit. People were stuck in elevators all the time. It was way overcrowded, but the shows were quick so before anybody could complain, it was over."

The designers agreed that an organized series of events was indeed a vast improvement upon the current conditions. Many industry meetings followed to discuss the new plan. One pivotal meeting was held at the 500 Club. Some of the younger designers questioned whether or not they would participate. They asked if Calvin Klein would be showing there. Fern Mallis had Klein, who was sitting in the front row, address them directly. He told them he was absolutely going to be there because they needed to do this together. That meeting was a turning point in the process.

Mallis and Stan Herman spent a year and a half testing the idea in venues around the city. Herman was on the board of directors of Bryant Park. He felt the park was the best location for the shows. After meeting with Mayor David Dinkins (in his tennis whites!) at Gracie Mansion, Bryant Park was officially named the new home of New York Fashion Week.

The doors of the Bryant Park tents opened on October 31, 1993. Supermodels like Cindy, Linda, Christy, and Naomi walked the runways, ushering in a new era of New York fashion that put the city on par with Paris and Milan. Over the years, the tents saw marriage proposals on the runway, designers hit in the face with pies, hurricanes, goats running for cover, models falling, anniversaries, retirements, fights, first ladies, charity events, celebrities, and so much more. The tents at Bryant Park were more than a venue. For a designer showing there for the first time, it was a sign that they had made it; they were now a part of the New York fashion community. For so many others, New York Fashion Week was, and remains, a welcome opportunity to catch up with friends and colleagues every few months.

During the years that became known as the Bryant Park Era, Eleanor Lambert's vision from the 1940s crystallized into a modern-day golden age for the fashion industry in New York. Spring 2011 saw a new era begin as the shows moved uptown, to Lincoln Center, bringing fashion together with the arts in a fitting union. Fashion insiders and followers across the world will bear witness to the evolution of the new venue and its place in the history of the industry.

The move from Bryant Park has become an opportunity for some to question the need for fashion shows as we know them. With the popularity of shows being streamed live on the web, there is a contingent that feels going digital is the wave of the future. Why should editors trek uptown to Lincoln Center, when they can see the same show on their computers in their offices? Only time will tell what the future of the fashion show will be. Nevertheless, we can always look back at the time when it all began, and be awestruck by the spectacle of fashion that showed under the tents of Bryant Park.

Linda Evangelista and Christy Turlington backstage at Anna Sui

SPRING/SUMMER
1994
THE FIRST SEASON
PRESENTED OCTOBER-NOVEMBER, 1993

TRENDS:
ATHLETIC

A SPORTY MOOD was in the air with the Lillehammer Olympics just months away. The athletic look was perfect for the supermodels that ushered in New York Fashion Week at Bryant Park.

Norma Kamali

DKNY

SLIP DRESSES

THIS TREND HAS roots in lingerie; however, for Spring 1994 it was anything but dainty. In a nod to grunge, the slip was typically layered over a T-shirt or a flannel shirt tied at the waist, and even paired with combat boots.

Richard Tyler, model: Ève Salvail

Todd Oldham, model: Cindy Crawford

CROPPED TOPS

THE CROPPED TOP reflects the changing of the female silhouette as women started working out as seriously as men. Female hardbodies were emerging, and designers were showing stylish ways of showing off six-pack abs with the cropped top.

Tyra Banks for Todd Oldham

Hair at Kalinka

ck's men

OTHER
HIGHLIGHTS

Todd Oldham's patterns

shoes and socks at ck

THE SCENE

* October 31, 1993 was the start date of the first Fashion Week at Bryant Park. Mayor David Dinkins missed the ribbon-cutting ceremony, but his wife Joyce was there to take his place.

* Donna Karan's DKNY was the first show ever in the tents.

* Cotton, Inc. chose four young designers to show their lines: Michael Leva, Stephen DiGeronimo, Sarah Phillips, and Zang Toi all showed courtesy of the company.

* Richard Tyler made his debut designing for Anne Klein.

* Tracy Reese's 1930s-inspired Magaschoni show was a hit with the crowd. The show opened with a trio of brass musicians and show goers enjoyed the added spectacle of slides of pastime jazz greats.

* A mistake at Mark Eisen's show resulted in a number of buyers and reporters denied admission.

* Betsey Johnson had a special delivery on the runway. To introduce her new shoe collection she had a FedEx man bring a shipment to the runway.

* Each seat at Donna Karan's show was equipped with headlamps to add light to her reflective clothing. Just before the show began an announcement was made to activate the light sources.

* Christy Turlington made news backstage when she got bangs cut.

* A brave Turlington modeled for Anne Klein with a broken toe.

* Christy Turlington was so unhappy when she saw photographer Steve Wood at the Ghost after party that she went over and kicked him. Word was she was upset because Wood allegedly took nude photos of her backstage without her permission.

Calvin Klein

Donna Karan's reflective clothes

Christy Turlington

Russell Simmons

Anna Wintour, Diane von Furstenburg, Tracy Pollan, and Michael J Fox

Backstage at Betsey Johnson

SNAPPED!

Ru Paul

Geoffrey Beene

STAN HERMAN

Stan Herman is a three-time Coty American Fashion Critic's award-winning designer. He served as president of the Council of Fashion Designers of America (CFDA) for sixteen years and was president of the 7th on Sixth Corporation for seven years. Herman has worked extensively for animal rights, pushing for the use of faux fur and raising funds to benefit the Central Park Zoo. He received lifetime achievement awards from the Dallas Market for his career in fashion, from the GMHC for his pioneering efforts in the fight against HIV/AIDS, and from the CFDA for his commitment to the advancement of American Fashion.

EILA MELL: What was it like getting the Bryant Park concept off the ground?

STAN HERMAN: Fern [Mallis] and I were the two spearheads for the tents. I was president of the CFDA at the time. It was a very benign organization up to that point. As president I really wanted it to be a working organization. Fern was the perfect executive director. She looked for the camera, and that's the way it should work. I became, in a sense, the guy behind it—as I preferred.

We began to talk to people about organizing. We realized we had to get sponsorship. I'm on the board of Bryant Park. More and more I thought the park was where we should be. New York City's strange. There are no big open spaces. We talked about other places, but this just seemed right. It's a magical park. It's very special.

We just pitched two tents. I called them bar mitzvah tents. They were sweet. When I see old pictures of them I get a nostalgic tear in my eye. And the beautiful part about it was it was so novel that all the A-list designers decided to join in. I'll never forget Calvin Klein and Donna Karan's faces when we showed them the plans for the tents. They saw it was a reality and became a part of it.

I remember walking Oscar de la Renta, Ralph Lauren, and Donna Karan through the tents when we first set them up. They were so excited. Nobody in America knew what a tent was. They thought it was something you went camping in. We go in and there's a city there. They were shocked. Even the most sophisticated people were shocked. It was a big thing. I was very proud.

EM: What do you think of the move to Lincoln Center?

SH: Lincoln Center was more electronic, smarter, easier. It lost that high-school diploma feel we always had. I liked it. I thought the outside was brilliant. The fashion junkies didn't show up like they did at Bryant Park. That was a big difference. We had all the lookers from 42nd Street at Bryant Park. This is 42nd Street, the heartbeat of America. Lincoln Center is culture. It's a big difference.

FRESH FACE

TRISH GOFF

FROM: PITTSBURGH, PENNSYLVANIA | HEIGHT: 5'9" | HAIR: BROWN | EYES: BROWN

"My first show ever at Bryant Park was for Anna Sui. I showed up a few hours before, and was the only one there for two and a half hours. They had all the names up on the racks. It was Naomi, Christy, Linda, Kate. I thought, 'No. It can't be them. Why would I suddenly be with them?' I said to Thomas, who worked for Anna Sui, 'I think you've made a mistake. I don't think I should be here.' He said, 'We haven't made a mistake, we want you here.'

"I'd never been on a catwalk and I'd never even worn heels before. I go to my first outfit and the shoes are massive platforms. I was the least important person in this fashion show so if someone's heels didn't fit they would put me in the smaller pair. Suddenly my shoes were two sizes too small in addition to being sky high. I thought, 'I'm going to get to the end of that catwalk and get back as fast as I can.' And that's what I did for every one of my outfits. I just zoomed down. I got back and I thought, 'I never want to do this again. This was nerve wracking.' I was retiring."

TRISH GOFF

Model Trish Goff made her runway debut at New York Fashion Week, walking exclusively for Anna Sui. She has appeared on the covers of *Vogue*, *Elle*, and *Marie Claire*, and has modeled in campaigns for Chanel, Louis Vuitton, and Yves Saint Laurent.

EILA MELL: You worked with Steven Meisel very early in your career. What was that like?

TRISH GOFF: My agency sent Steven Meisel pictures and he called and asked to see me for a story in *Vogue Italia*. I still had a night job as a hostess in a restaurant. It was Christmas time. I was basically living on people's couches. I was sixteen and really struggling to survive in New York without living off my agency. I had told the restaurant I was eighteen in order to even get that job.

The day of the Steven Meisel shoot I had to be at the restaurant at 4:30. The day started getting on and Steven hadn't shot me that much. I told Gary, the hairstylist, "If he wants to get a picture of me he should do it soon because I have to leave at 4:00." He asked where I was going and I said I had to go to work. He said, "But you are at work." People were saying that I can't just leave a Steven Meisel shoot, but I told them that I *was* leaving at 4:00, that I would get fired if I didn't. I told Steven if he wanted to shoot me he had to do it immediately because if I didn't work I wouldn't be able to get home for Christmas. Steven knew I was just being completely honest with him and he understood. He worked with me right away and he let me go at 4:00. When I left he told me he would see me again in the new year, and when he did I wouldn't have a night job anymore. I didn't understand the level of it. I was completely naïve. It was ignorance all the way.

EM: What was it like working in the supermodel era?

TG: It was the golden era of modeling. I came in at the end of that time. I will never forget always feeling like the baby. I was tiny. These girls were curvaceous and gorgeous. I was so skinny they had to redo clothes to get them on me. When you look at old pictures of Versace shows, the models were so beautiful. That's what women wanted to be like.

EM: How has modeling changed since you started?

TG: When I started Anna Wintour would not put me in American *Vogue* because she said I wasn't a woman and I hadn't worked enough. I didn't have enough experience so I had to wait. American *Vogue* didn't sell to sixteen year olds. Even if they made me look twenty that wasn't the audience. The audience was twenty-five to forty. I didn't fit in that. Linda Evangelista fit in it. When I made it there I was so happy. I'd been in everything else, but this was my marker. Then I would laugh and say *Vogue* should put me on salary because I was in it every week. But it was earned. I think that's a really big thing because now young girls get in so quickly. They do these top things immediately and then suddenly a season later they'll only do two shows a day. I did six to eight shows a day for ten years.

Another big change is on the runway. There used to be a guy, J. Alexander from *America's Next Top Model*. He would teach you how to walk because you had to do things on the runway, like take things off. Now you don't need to do that. I remember J. always said to me, "You're like a black panther walking down that catwalk. They can't touch you; you're dangerous." We used to have to stop, sometimes three times on the catwalk, do a turn, take something off. We used to have five outfits a show. You had to know what you were doing.

DKNY

FALL/WINTER
1994
A COLORFUL SEASON
PRESENTED APRIL 1994

TRENDS:
PLAID

FALL 1994'S PLAID was no Highland fling. This was a reflection of grunge, which was at its peak.

DKNY

Badgley Mischka

TWINSETS

TWINSETS WERE AN easy way to have a pulled-together look without wearing a suit. At this point suit jackets had mostly disappeared from the runways.

COLOR

BRIGHT WAS RIGHT for Fall/Winter 1994.

DKNY, model: Shalom Harlow

Badgley Mischka

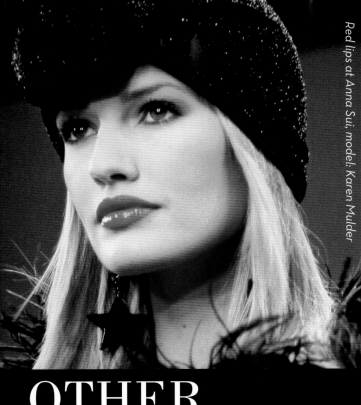

OTHER HIGHLIGHTS

THE SCENE

Douglas Keeve followed Isaac Mizrahi with a camera backstage at Fashion Week. Keeve was making the documentary *Unzipped*, which chronicled the creation and showing of Mizrahi's Fall/Winter 1994 collection.

Prescriptives launched their fall palette, Color 95, on the runways. They provided makeup artists and assistants with their new colors for use in the shows.

Not only did Todd Oldham debut a new line, but he also showed off a streamlined new physical appearance as well. Oldham had recently dropped fifteen pounds after deciding to eliminate animal products from his diet.

The accessories industry joined the crowd at the tents. *Stripes of the Tiger*, a sixteen-minute film which illustrated the importance of the category was shown followed by a parade of accessories designers.

Some parties were really hard to get into. Helena Christensen was denied entrance to a party that she was co-hosting.

Bill Blass, Miuccia Prada, Carolina Herrera, Arnold Scaasi, Yeohlee, and Isabel Toledo showed at the tents after being absent from season one.

Escada had its first U.S. runway show at the Celeste Bartos Library. Robert Leacock, who was the director of photography for Madonna's documentary *Truth or Dare*, shot a behind-the-scenes video that played during the show. Leacock's video was in 3D, and show goers such as Burt Tansky, Joan Kaner, and Etta Froio obediently sat in the front row wearing their paper glasses.

Special Appearance: Sofia Coppola walking for Donna Karan Collection.

Sofia Coppola

Todd Oldham

Carla Bruni

BARBARA BERMAN

Barbara Berman has been dressing models for New York Fashion Week since 1994. In addition, Berman has also worked behind the scenes at high profile events such as the Macy's Thanksgiving Day Parade, the Daytime Emmys, and the Country Music Awards.

EILA MELL: How did you get involved with New York Fashion Week?

BARBARA BERMAN: While attending NYU for my certification in Entertainment Marketing, I was invited by one of my event planning professors to observe Fashion Week the first time all the shows were brought under one roof in Bryant Park. I was immediately hooked and became a volunteer during its second season.

EM: What does your job entail?

BB: I coordinate dressing services for designers and producers. I work with the styling team to be sure that all the looks are executed properly and the show will run smoothly. I also recruit and train dressers and supervisors.

EM: What is it like backstage?

BB: Backstage is full of energy. This is the moment designers have been working toward and all pieces must be in place by show time.

EM: What are some of your favorite memories from the shows?

BB: I loved working on the Isaac Mizrahi show while he was filming *Unzipped*. The last season at Bryant Park was bittersweet but memorable. I loved the closing party. It was a slice of history.

EM: What are some of the more unusual things you've seen backstage?

BB: I've seen designers still sewing their collections after the show has started. I've seen dresses arrive by taxi after the show has started and they make it onto the runway. I've seen models arrive after the show has started, get full hair and makeup, and still make their exit!

EM: How has Fashion Week changed since you started?

BB: Fashion Week has become more heavily sponsored and thus more about the sponsors. Fashion Week shows have also become the basis for episodes of reality TV.

EM: What's the most fun part of your job?

BB: I love when we execute fast changes flawlessly. I also enjoy knowing I've been part of making a designer's collection come to life on the runway. It's extremely rewarding—like being part of live theater.

EM: What would people be surprised to know about New York Fashion Week?

BB: People would be surprised to know that Fashion Week is not profitable for designers. It is a marketing tool. They would also be surprised to know that the clothes seen on the runway are not always manufactured.

FRESH
FACE

KIRSTY HUME

FROM: AYRSHIRE, SCOTLAND | HEIGHT: 5'11" | HAIR: BLONDE | EYES: BLUE

PHILLIP BLOCH

Celebrity stylist Phillip Bloch has dressed some of world's biggest celebrities, including Sandra Bullock, Nicole Kidman, Salma Hayek, Jennifer Lopez, and Michael Jackson. Bloch has worked as a contributing editor for *InStyle* magazine, and is author of the books *Elements of Style* and *The Shopping Diet*.

EILA MELL: Were you at New York Fashion Week the first season it was in Bryant Park?

PHILLIP BLOCH: I guess I was. At the beginning of your career you're wide eyed and bushy tailed. You feel like you've stepped into this society—like you're the littlest star trying to sparkle in the galaxy. I didn't realize it was the beginning of it all. I thought it all existed without me because you grow up knowing Donna Karan, Calvin Klein, Oscar de la Renta, and all the names. It just seemed like it was all organized before you got there. Who knew?

EM: What's it like styling a fashion show?

PB: You're taking something fashionable and making it commercial. It's a great job if you have the stomach for it. The timing is very intense; it's all happening in a few days. You're fighting over getting the right models. At the last minute everything that can go wrong will go wrong. But it's a very interesting job to take someone else's creation and put your spin on it. The designer creates a collection but then the stylist comes in and recreates it. They get six months to do whatever they're doing. You get about a couple of days to make it all make sense and then make it not only commercial, but editorially interesting.

EM: How did celebrities come to have such a presence at the shows?

PB: Celebrities at Fashion Week grew. It came into play mostly at the end of the 1990s. It became unbearable to the people who actually make a living in the business. Editors got tired of waiting for shows to start because a certain celebrity hadn't gotten there yet. They have a job to do. Everything in fashion is cyclical. This too shall pass.

EM: You were one of the first celebrity stylists, if not the first.

PB: I was the one to connect New York and Hollywood. When I got to Hollywood, Versace and Armani were the only two with any liaison there. I basically was the conduit between fashion houses and publicists and clients. It was mutually beneficial.

EM: How were you received at Fashion Week?

PB: I remember in Fall/Winter 1994 there were all these women, the Carrie Donovans—that more mature group. They were ruling the roost in those days. Ellen Saltzman was on one side of me and a lot of the other women were on the other. She turns to me and just says, "Who are you and what do you do and what is the fuss all about?" She's this really chic woman that I've seen and I know roughly who she is. I was just mortified. I'm a stylist from Los Angeles. There was a disdain underneath, but because she's a great woman it was interesting. It was an insiders club really, and I suddenly made it public. I'm this garish Long Island kid who lives in Hollywood, who dresses movie stars and cameras are following me. Commotion ensued everywhere I went. I guess some people might say when I started going to the shows it started to lose its glamour. I thought I was bringing a little flavor to it!

EM: How have the shows changed over the years?

PB: Now we have so many bloggers and pictures. I want a dollar for every picture I take. I would love to know where all those pictures go. Now it's like a trade show. Everybody has their cameras, their video cameras, their blog, their show. People are Tweeting from the front row.

SNAPPED!

Fashion Targets Breast Cancer

Ivana Trump

Anna Wintour

Bjork

Shalom Harlow and Issac Mizrahi

SPRING/SUMMER
1995
A LADYLIKE SEASON
PRESENTED NOVEMBER 1994

TRENDS: SUITS

SPRING/SUMMER 1995 saw a resurgence of the suit. This was the return of the lady at a time when people were dressing up more.

Bill Blass

Ralph Lauren, model: Yasmeen Ghauri

SHINE

WHILE WE HAD seen shine before, this time around the industry experimented with new techniques utilizing a variety of fabrics.

Anna Sui

Isaac Mizrahi

1940s

THIS WAS A disco glam version of the 1940s with glittery makeup, whimsical prints, and vintage-style clothing.

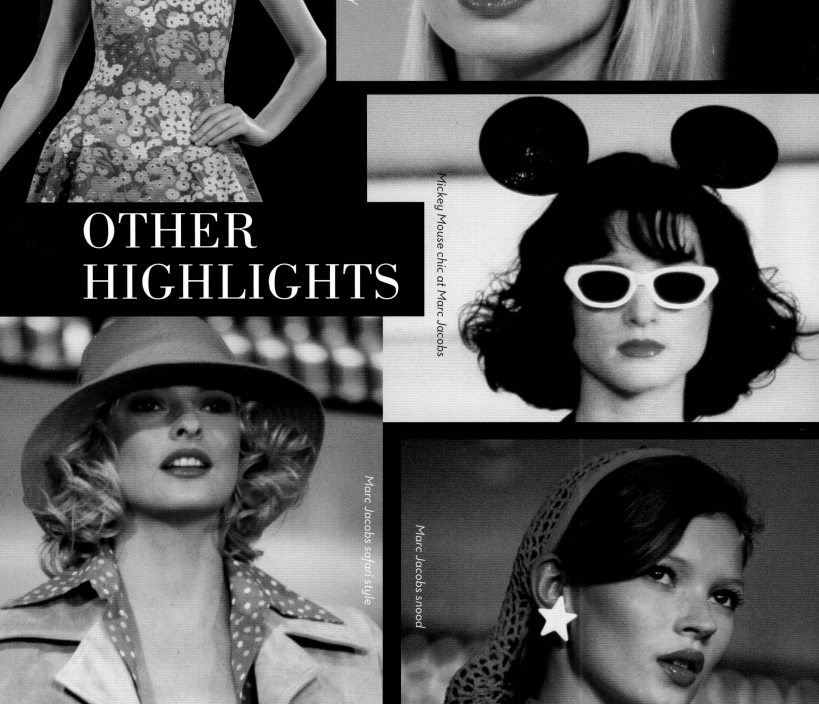

Isaac Mizrahi's bathing beauty

DKNY

OTHER HIGHLIGHTS

Mickey Mouse chic at Marc Jacobs

Marc Jacobs safari style

Marc Jacobs snood

THE SCENE

★ Instead of a runway show, a very pregnant Jennifer George made a video instead. A few hours after sending out the tapes George gave birth to a daughter. The name of the video—"It's a Girl."

★ Label by Laura Whitcomb was originally set to show in the tents. Then Whitcomb decided to change the location to Studio 54. She then canceled the show, reportedly because she didn't think her samples would arrive in time. They did arrive, and Whitcomb went on with the show at Studio 54.

★ Tracy Feith chose an unusual locale for his show—New York City's biggest and flashiest porn palace, Show World Center. Model Beri Smither decided against appearing in the show.

★ Show goers could have salt water taffy with their fashion as Lance Karesh had his Basco show at Howard Johnson's in Times Square.

★ Cotton Inc. had their second show. The designers they sponsored this season were Heidi Weisel, Eric Gaskins, Sophia Tezel, and Sylvia Heisel.

★ Bianca Jagger showed up for the Calvin Klein show a day early.

★ Unknown designer Kara Saun staged a renegade fashion show on the steps of Bryant Park.

Bianca Jagger and Calvin Klein

Kate Moss

Niki Taylor

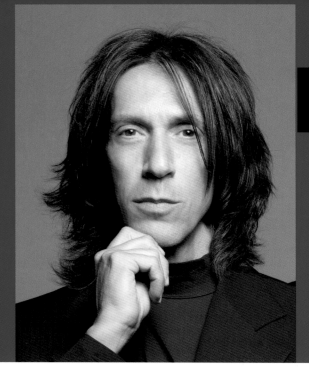

EDWARD TRICOMI

Legendary hairstylist Edward Tricomi has worked backstage at Fashion Week since the very beginning. His work has been in the pages of magazines such as *Vogue* and *W*. In 1996 Tricomi and business partner Joel Warren opened the Warren-Tricomi salon at the Plaza Hotel.

EILA MELL: What was the first season you styled hair for New York Fashion Week?

EDWARD TRICOMI: It was in 1970 for Geoffrey Beene. Back then, fashion shows were intimate and small. The shows were held in showrooms where buyers came to look at the collection in a presentation setting. In 1979 the shows started to get bigger and bigger and crazier and crazier.

EM: Are there designers you work with every season?

ET: Yes, I work with Douglas Hannant, Anne Bowen, and Rosa Cha each season, but I've worked on every show imaginable—Calvin Klein, Ralph Lauren, Vera Wang, you name it.

EM: What is the working relationship like between you and the designer?

ET: It's a great collaborative between the designer and I. The designer has a certain vision in mind and together we come up with the hairstyle, but I sometimes have some of my own ideas when I see the collection. When we did the Carolina Herrera bridal show we created twenty-one different hairstyles, which was really difficult to do, and I had to be responsible for each and every look.

EM: How many stylists are on your team for Fashion Week?

ET: It really depends on the number of models. The general rule of thumb is three models for every one hair dresser/makeup artist.

EM: What are some of the more unusual things you've seen at the tents?

ET: Definitely fashion wannabes and groupies—you can't distinguish their outfits from Halloween or fashion. In the late 1970s, people would get dressed for Halloween and they wouldn't look any different from getting dressed for the week. It does make it exciting though, that people dress up and try to do things differently and it's fun to see what their interpretation is of certain styles.

EM: How long does it usually take to get a model's hair ready for a show?

ET: It really depends on the look. Sometimes it can take three minutes, sometimes it can take forty-five minutes.

EM: Is there a cut that's flattering to most women?

ET: Layers that frame the face are flattering on most women.

EM: How has NY Fashion Week changed over the years?

ET: It has gotten better and better and keeps improving every year. It became more organized as designers and industry insiders became more experienced with putting on these shows. Europe has always done it big and New York is right up there as one of the biggest, most exciting Fashion Weeks. That's what we want and what we deserve. We're a billion-dollar industry and we deserve the spotlight.

EM: Do you voice your opinion if you think that what the designer has asked for isn't the best option?

ET: Yes, I am very frank, but if the designer wants it a certain way they'll get it. They have the last say—it's their show.

EM: What happens when models come in late for a show?

ET: You rush like hell to get them together. The worst is when they come in with gel in their hair and you have to wash the hair and blow it out. It wastes precious time.

EM: Being such an iconic hairstylist, do you ever find that designers look to you for hair ideas?

ET: Absolutely, they ask me all the time. Designers call up and ask for a test run. They get a model and the designer has some inspiration of what they want to do with the show, whether it's 1940s inspiration, space odyssey, etc. They take that inspiration and look at the clothes and figure out whether the clothes would best be served with small or linear heads, big hair, etc., and then you design the shape and flavor that the hair will have. It's about creating living art and subtle nuances whether it's a curl or a braid. A lot of thought process goes into the hairdo. What we do inspires the rest of the country and each person interprets it a little differently. Celebrities start wearing it and everyone catches on. New York is always ahead of the trends; we're creating the fashions that everyone is copying.

EM: What would people be surprised to know about NY Fashion Week?

ET: That we can actually accomplish twenty to twenty-five different looks in the limited time that we have.

RALPH RUCCI

Designer and artist Ralph Rucci launched his line in 1994. He is known for his flawless construction and his use of luxurious fabrics. In 2002 Rucci became the first American designer in nearly seventy years to be invited to show at Paris Haute Couture under his own name. He was given the Artistry of Fashion Award from the Couture Council of the Museum at FIT and the Fashion Icon award from the Pratt Institute.

EILA MELL: Did you always want to be a designer?

RALPH RUCCI: It didn't hit me until I was in college. I was studying philosophy and painting on the side. I was writing a paper, and in the stacks of the library I came across David Bailey photographs. One was called "A Bride," and it was a white trapezoidal shape. The other was her attendant in a black trapezoidal shape. When I saw them that was the moment—because I realized you could make clothes and they can relate to fine art because they looked like something from Robert Motherwell's *Elegies to the Spanish Republic*. I immediately and voraciously began to research. I became obsessed with fashion. I bought fabric and a sewing machine. I started to teach myself. I cut right into the fabric. I began to sew and drape things on my sister. I went through images in old issues of *Vogue* and I discovered Balenciaga. Then I discovered there was a man in New York who had also been very influenced by Balenciaga. His name was Halston. I ran through college in three years and then I came to New York. I only wanted to work for Halston. I knocked on his door and got a job in the studio. That was in 1977.

EM: Does your background in philosophy and art influence your work?

RR: I give myself into work that is intellectually stimulating. This is my life. There is no difference between my work and me. The art is very significant. My paintings are often screened onto fabrics. We do that in Como or in Switzerland. The philosophy is also very important because it gives us a handle on how to approach women evolving in society that want a sense of style and taste, disregarding the phobia of the moment. If something is so current it's phobic to us because it means it's over as soon as it hits. The questions of what makes something timeless are always part of our work. I say our—my team, is extraordinary. I'm the only designer here. My pattern makers are my team.

EM: What was it like showing your collection for the first time?

RR: The first time I ever showed was 1980, at the Old Westbury Hotel at 69th and Madison. It was an all-bias collection—an homage to Madame Grés. I had a teeny one-room apartment on 71st Street. We had no budget for anything. We didn't even have carting service. I wheeled the rack of clothes from my apartment to Madison Avenue. Sometimes I sneak a pattern from that collection and cut it in a new fabric and put it in a new collection. Everybody always asks about it. That whole first collection I made with my own hands. It's very personal for me.

EM: One of your early supporters was Neiman Marcus's Joan Kaner.

RR: She was the Fashion Director at Neiman Marcus for many years. She came up to my little shoebox showroom at 550 7th Avenue. She couldn't get Neiman Mar-

His collections are so aspirational and inspirational.
I'm always impressed with his construction and technique. His sheer ingenuity takes my breath away—a sumptuous sable suspended on chiffon defies gravity and elevates craftsmanship to a new level."

—Glenda Bailey

cus to look at my collection because nobody knew who I was. So she said she wanted to order a wardrobe all in black and chocolate brown to take to Europe. We did it right away. This is how Joan Kaner got people to come look at me. I always say she's my Carmel Snow. Carmel was an editor-in-chief at *Harper's Bazaar*. There was a Spaniard in Paris who was showing clothes that no one was looking at. It wasn't until Carmel Snow gave him something like eleven pages that people said, "Who is this Balenciaga?" Joan retired. I miss her.

EM: How has fashion changed since you started?

RR: When I entered the profession there were so many fashion houses, and dozens of contracting shops with extraordinarily skilled workers—Bill Blass, Pauline Trigère, Geoffrey Beene, Halston. The most extraordinary clothes were made in New York City, and we had an industry. We no longer have that. Those shops are gone. Over the years I've had to figure out how we can continue to make our clothes, so I put together our own in-house production department. Everything we make is under my own roof and then shipped. It's insanely costly. That's why it's not ordinarily done like that today. Some days I don't even know how I do it. The industry has evolved in being much more tied together with China and other parts of the world. We no longer have an industry here in America that allows skilled workers to get jobs. Who would they work for?

EM: You recently showed in your showroom. What was that like?

RR: It was a magical experience. Those who were invited not only got to see the collection, but they were able to see the enormous variety of people that are part of this, from Patti Smith sitting next to Martha Stewart.

EM: What was it like being one of the only American designers ever to show at the Paris couture shows?

RR: That's a special thing to me. Paris is a bed of creativity. I always called it the Vatican of fashion. It was the supreme honor. When we began doing it I was terrified. This was a major undertaking. The collection was received incredibly, and we found ourselves in the haute couture business.

EM: You choose not to participate in red carpet dressing. Any particular reason?

RR: I've felt a great disappointment seeing this industry succumb to lending clothes to starlets and to people as a venue for selling clothes. When a stylist calls here and just expects something to be hung on a rack to be chosen with twenty other garments, I say no. I'm disrespecting my clothes when I do that. If an actress calls here and she wishes to purchase something, great. But I'm not part of that conveyer belt of the red carpet.

EM: What were your days in Bryant Park like?

RR: I've always said that Bryant Park was a fantastic organization. I adored the super organization that Fern brought to it. That whole team there was terrific to work with. They made it very easy for people to see clothes in America. I loved showing there.

FRESH FACE

CHRYSTELE SAINT LOUIS AUGUSTIN

FROM: PARIS, FRANCE | HEIGHT: 5'10" | HAIR: BROWN | EYES: BLUE

Marilu Henner &
David Lee Roth

Mickey Rourke

Carolina Herrera

SNAPPED!

Kristen McMenamy

Carré Otis & Mark Eisen

Carla Bruni

Bill Blass, model: Trish Goff

FALL/WINTER
1995
A DARK SEASON
PRESENTED APRIL 1995

MASCULINE/FEMININE

FALL/WINTER 1995 presented the fashion world with a continuation of the suiting trend from the previous season, but at a more fitting time of year for a suit. This was a softer take on the masculine trend. It was most decidedly not the power suit of the 1980s.

Richard Tyler

Joop

BLACK

PERHAPS AS A reaction to last season's colors, designers went back to the New York uniform of black. In a dark season like this, black was the predominant shade and mood.

Geoffrey Beene

Todd Oldham, model: Helena Christensen

MOD

DESIGNERS HAD FUN with mod this season. There was a play on 1960s British culture seen on the runways. We saw black-and-white, graphics, and shift dresses, mostly worn with boots. This appealed more to the fashion consumer than to the average shopper.

icole Mill

Nicole Miller's Leather

OTHER HIGHLIGHTS

Joop's sunglasses

Strapless at Calvin Klein

THE SCENE

★ Supermodels were scarce on the runway this season. Claudia Schiffer and Cindy Crawford were noticeably absent, while Kate Moss, Linda Evangelista, and Naomi Campbell made few appearances.

★ All of New York City was invited to Cynthia Rowley's show—sort of. The designer decided to give everyone a peek at the goings on in the tents, and broadcast her show on the Jumbotron in Times Square.

★ Naomi Campbell, Claudia Schiffer, and Elle Macpherson opened the Fashion Café. The theme restaurant showed fashion shows while the customers dined, leaving many to wonder how many diners ordered dessert after watching the models walk the runways.

★ Each model/founder of Fashion Café added a special item to the menu from their home country. England's Naomi Campbell had fish and chips while Claudia Schiffer's dish was a German pancake. Elle Macpherson's addition was the very Australian spicy shrimp on the barbie.

★ Fashion Café's opening was in the style of a movie premiere, with crowds and photographers. Malcolm McLaren, David Copperfield, and fellow model Veronica Webb showed up to lend their support.

★ Special Appearances: Isabella Rossellini and Steven Tyler walking for Betsey Johnson.

Isabella Rossellini

Steven Tyler

GLENDA BAILEY

Glenda Bailey was born in Derbyshire, England and earned her degree in fashion from Kingston University. In the early 1980s she produced a collection for Italian designer Guisi Slaviero before starting her career in publishing. She has worked as editor for the magazines *Honey* and *FOLIO*, and she launched *British Marie Claire* in 1988. She earned three Magazine Editor of the Year awards, five Magazine of the Year awards, and two Amnesty International awards. In 2001, Bailey became editor in chief of *Harper's Bazaar*. In 2008 she was appointed as an Officer of the Order of the British Empire (OBE).

EILA MELL: What do you look for in a collection to feature in the pages of *Harper's Bazaar*?

GLENDA BAILEY: It's all about the readers—their needs and their desires. When we look at the collections, we look to whether designers have produced a show that their customers are going to love and to want to buy. Then, we feature the looks that are going to appeal to our readers and give suggestions and solutions for their fashion needs.

EM: What is your favorite part of NY Fashion Week?

GB: The clothes and the accessories.

EM: How is Fashion Week in New York different from those in other cities?

GB: American designers are so incredibly talented, and it's thrilling to see their vision for the next season. In New York, it's great to see new designers showing—it adds vibrancy and excitement to the week.

FRESH FACES

FARRAH SUMMERFORD

FROM: NASHVILLE, TENESSEE | HEIGHT: 5'11" | HAIR: BLONDE | EYES: GREEN

IRINA PANTAEVA

FROM: ULAN-UDE, SIBERIA | HEIGHT: 5'10" | HAIR: BLACK | EYES: BROWN

ÈVE SALVAIL

Ève Salvail was one of the top models of the 1990s. Her success led to roles in films such as *The Fifth Element* and *Zoolander*. Salvail has changed direction in her career, and has become a high-profile celebrity DJ.

EILA MELL: How did you get into modeling?

ÈVE SALVAIL: I was discovered by Jean Paul Gaultier and from there my modeling career blew up.

EM: What was your first New York show like?

ES: I think it was a Spring/Summer collection in the early 1990s. Joan Vass was the first American designer to bring me to the U.S. It was so exciting and I loved working with her. I loved her eccentric ways.

EM: Is there a difference working with a veteran designer as opposed to a new one?

ES: From my perspective, the young designers are out shooting for the stars and have nothing to lose, whereas established designers have so much more pressure to perform up to, or better, than their prior performance.

EM: What is the relationship between model and designer like?

ES: The model is expressing and representing the designer's inspiration and vision of the collection that season. On a more personal level, designers live and breathe fashion and their next collection, so naturally there is a "muse"-like quality to the relationship between the designer and the few chosen models.

EM: How does Fashion Week in New York compare to those in other cities?

ES: New York is the most organized of all the cities. Paris is insane, but each city has its own Fashion Week flavor.

EM: Has modeling changed much since you were involved?

ES: My time as a model was the era of the "supermodels," and it's no longer that way. Now designers and designs have taken back the limelight.

EM: You have such fantastic personal style. Were you ever pressured to change it as a model?

ES: Thank you. The hair was always a big issue because everybody wanted a different look at the last minute, but otherwise not really.

EM: What would people be surprised to know about models?

ES: Some are very smart!

EM: What's the most enjoyable part of Fashion Week?

ES: Being part of Fashion Week in New York, my favorite city in the world, was the biggest deal ever.

EM: What are some of the more unusual things you've seen at NY Fashion Week?

ES: Sex, drugs, and rock and roll! Wait, can I say that?

EM: What's your take on the skinny model issue?

ES: I think curves are beautiful. However, I understand that at times the designer's vision requires a skinnier model to present the collection. Still, I'm saddened by some of the tragic repercussions of the industry.

EM: Is there a designer who was your favorite to work with?

ES: I loved them all, but my all-time favorite was Jean Paul Gaultier because we worked so closely for so long and had a special bond.

Marisa Berenson

Calvin Klein

7 SEVENTH ON SALE
THE RETURN TO NEW YORK

SNAPPED!

Issac Mizrahi

GHOST

Ghost

SPRING/SUMMER

1996

THE EUROPEAN INVASION

PRESENTED NOVEMBER 1995

TRENDS: DRESSES

Betsey Johnson

DKNY

SIMPLICITY

A NEW MINIMALISM appeared on the runways. There were no visible details (hidden buttons, zippers, etc.), no logos. An austere moment took hold.

Calvin Klein Collection, model: Michele Hicks

Calvin Klein Collection, model: Kate Moss

LOW SLUNG

HERE WE HAVE the beginning of the crack attack. Pants and skirts started to lay on the hip a bit more. This was influenced by the wave of waif models led by Kate Moss.

OTHER HIGHLIGHTS

Soft waves at Ralph Lauren, model: Elaine Irwin

Todd Oldham's sandals

Todd Oldham's updo, model: Carolyn Murphy

★ Kate Moss was reportedly upset by a *New York Daily News* story which stated that designers were over booking supermodels for their shows. Moss compared it to reading her own obituary.

★ Italian designer Gianni Versace brought his show to New York this season. Versace was one of a group of European designers showing in Bryant Park, which worried some American designers who feared they would be overshadowed. However, Fern Mallis said the situation was under control; the American designers would still make up at least 90 percent of the shows.

★ A date with *New York* magazine writer Michael Musto was auctioned off for $400 at a DIFFA benefit hosted by Carol Alt. DIFFA (Design Industries Foundation Fighting AIDS) is one of the country's largest supporters of direct care for people living with HIV/AIDS and preventative education for those at risk.

★ Betsey Johnson got flak from the CFDA for showing at the Millennium Hotel instead of at Bryant Park. Ironically, the CFDA's opening party was held at the Millennium Hotel.

Kevyn Aucoin

Kate Moss

Betsey Johnson's show

DEAN SNYDER

Producer Dean Snyder, of Eyesight, has created shows for designers such as Zac Posen, Sophie Theallet, Miguel Adrover, and Christian Cota. His producing skills are in demand for about a dozen shows per season.

EILA MELL: Your job starts long before Fashion Week begins. What happens at the beginning?

DEAN SNYDER: The job is all encompassing. I have creative meetings with the designer and the stylist, then deal with PR, lighting, sets. A fashion show is not showing up and sending models down a runway. We deal with lawyers, architects, model agencies, permits, etc. We deal with every aspect of the show. You have to be a creative, business, and technical person. If you're doing a curtain it has to be exact. We have to put the same amount of detail in what we do as the designers put into the clothes.

EM: What is it like the week before Fashion Week?

DS: The week is insane. My team is with me for ten days. I get about eleven hours of sleep in seven days. We can't do our job if we're not organized beforehand. Everything has to be planned to the minute.

EM: What do you do during Fashion Week?

DS: I have to be at every show. I direct and work backstage.

EM: Is there a particular season that's more difficult?

DS: The February shows can be hard. We come back from Paris, and then there's Thanksgiving, Christmas, and New Year's, which gives us less time to prepare for the February shows. You also have to deal with the weather. There can be hurricanes, blizzards. One year there was a huge snowstorm the day before a load in. We had to bring in a hundred people to shovel. We've also done a show in a blizzard. We had to bring trucks in eight hours early to get there and then wait in front of the venue.

EM: What would people be surprised to know about New York Fashion Week?

DS: All this work and it's over in nine minutes.

FRESH FACES

AMIT MACHTINGER

FROM: TEL AVIV, ISRAEL | HEIGHT: 5'11"
HAIR: BROWN | EYES: BLUE

GUINEVERE VAN SEENUS

FROM: WASHINGTON, D.C. | HEIGHT: 5' 9½"
HAIR: BLONDE | EYES: BLUE

Donna Karan Collection

FALL/WINTER
1996
A SOFTER SEASON
PRESENTED MARCH 27–APRIL 2, 1996

TRENDS:
VELVET

A CLASSIC COOL-weather fabric, velvet was romantic for Fall 1996. It was soft, flowing, and had a regal feel.

Jill Stuart

Donna Karan Collection

LEATHER

DESIGNERS WERE ABLE to get leather softer than ever. This season leather was less utilitarian and more about craft.

SKIN

THIS TREND WAS about being sexy without being trashy. Cutouts in clothing focused the eyes on flashes of skin we wouldn't have noticed before, signaling new erogenous zones.

Bill Blass

Richard Tyler

OTHER
HIGHLIGHTS

Nicole Miller's glasses

Anna Sui's bird, model: Naomi Campbell

Cynthia Rowley's knits

Todd Oldham's plaid

Dark lips at Richard Tyler

Dark eyes at Isaac Mizrahi

ALEX LUNDQVIST

Alex Lundqvist's career took off when he was spotted by photographer Bruce Weber and Wilhelmina Models agent Sean Patterson in 1994. Almost immediately after, Lundqvist appeared in a Versace campaign shot by Weber. He quickly rose to become one of the world's most sought-after male models. Lundqvist appeared as Fergie's boyfriend in the video for her song "Clumsy." He divides his time between modeling and being a professional paintball player.

EILA MELL: How did you start modeling?

ALEX LUNDQVIST: I got scouted for an agency in Sweden called Mikas.

EM: Does a male model typically have a longer career than a female model?

AL: I think that is very individual depending on the model—Naomi, Linda, and the supermodels have had extensive careers . . . But it seems like there is a revival of more mature models, both male and female.

EM: What's the most fun part of modeling?

AL: To travel and work with some of the most creative people all over the world, from designers and photographers to art directors and stylists.

EM: What would people be surprised to know about New York Fashion Week?

AL: How chaotic it is behind the scenes.

THE SCENE

★ Cynthia Rowley's models had to share the runway this season. Rowley included real New York City firemen in her show.

★ More than a hundred people, including Anna Wintour, Isabella Blow, and André Leon Talley, had to wait outside in the sleet for more than thirty minutes to get into Alexander McQueen's show at a Lower East Side synagogue. According to the show's producer the reason for the delay was show crashers.

★ While in New York conservative politician Pat Buchanan tried to shut down the tents. *Women's Wear Daily* quoted Buchanan as saying the fashion shows were full of "bare-breasted women, sexual deviants, and Mediterranean types."

★ Calvin Klein was upset that some New York designers (namely Donna Karan and Ralph Lauren) decided to forego the tents this season in favor of other venues. Donna Karan stood by her decision. Karan said she was bothered by the amount of media at the shows. Ralph Lauren's fabric deliveries were late, which was his reason for changing the day and venue of his show. Lauren rescheduled to the first day of Passover, which inconvenienced some guests. Lauren publicly apologized to those who were put out, and explained that there were no available slots in the schedule.

★ There was big buzz at the tents about Donna Karan and Saks Fifth Avenue's initial public offerings.

★ Guests arriving at Fashion Week didn't have to worry about snacks. Bags of popcorn were given out upon entrance to the tents courtesy of Samsung. Word got around that Anna Wintour was not pleased with the aroma from the treat.

★ Few supermodels were seen on the runways. In their place was a new crop of skinnier, more androgynous models.

★ Special Appearance: Daisy Fuentes walking for Nicole Miller.

Isabella Blow

Daisy Fuentes at Nicole Miller

Donna Karan

JADE PARFITT

Jade's first runway walk was for Prada in Spring 1995. The following seasons saw her modeling for Chanel, Shiatzy Chen, Jasper Conran, Christian Dior, Jean Paul Gaultier, Karl Lagerfeld, and Alexander McQueen. In 2000, Jade started a charity called Clothesline with model and friend Jasmine Guinness. Clothesline was founded to raise money for people suffering as a result of the HIV/AIDS pandemic in sub-Saharan Africa.

EILA MELL: How did you get into modeling?

JADE PARFITT: When I was fifteen my mum entered me in a competition on a program called *This Morning* in the UK. Viewers had to phone in and vote for their favorites. I won a contract with Models 1.

EM: What was your first season at NY Fashion Week like?

JP: My first was also one of my busiest! I remember walking for Calvin Klein, Donna Karan, Badgley Mischka, Marc Jacobs, and others. It was exciting being in New York and working so hard. It went by in a bit of a blur. I remember being delighted that I was in a show with models like Linda Evangelista and Shalom Harlow, and being lucky enough to have Kevyn Aucoin do my makeup several times that week.

EM: What do you love most about modeling?

JP: If you make it as a model the best things undoubtedly are that you get to travel, make good money, and work with creative people.

EM: What is it like working with some of the best designers in the business?

JP: I have been very lucky throughout my career to have had great relationships and to have worked consistently with designers such as Jean Paul Gaultier, John Galliano, Ralph Rucci, and Alexander McQueen. I was fortunate enough to be involved in some very creative shows that sometimes asked more of the models than to simply walk the runway. In these instances the designer needs to be able to trust that you understand their vision and will be able to bring it to life in the way they imagined it. I danced for John Galliano, was the bride three times for Jean Paul Gaultier and was asked by Alexander McQueen to freak out during his show, "The Birds"—which I was also wearing in the show.

EM: What would people be surprised to know about NY Fashion Week?

JP: New York Fashion Week is pretty much the only Fashion Week where shows run on time! Typically businesslike, everyone, including the models, are paid by the hour so there are rarely any late arrivals, unlike in Europe.

FRESH
FACES

CHANDRA NORTH

FROM: DALLAS, TEXAS | HEIGHT: 5'9" |
HAIR: BROWN | EYES: BLUE

JODIE KIDD

FROM: CANTERBURY, ENGLAND
HEIGHT: 6' | HAIR: BLONDE | EYES: BLUE

TASHA TILBERG

FROM: CHILLIWACK, BRITISH COLUMBIA | HEIGHT: 5'9" | HAIR: BROWN | EYES: BLUE/GREEN

STACEY MCKENZIE

FROM: KINGSTON, JAMAICA | HEIGHT: 5'10" | HAIR: AUBURN | EYES: BROWN

"The first show I did at Bryant Park was Todd Oldham. Once my agent told me about the booking with him I cried. When my agent told me the show was being held at the famous Bryant Park I broke down completely bawling my eyes out! I'd arrived!"—Stacey McKenzie

SNAPPED!

Amber Valletta, Todd Oldham, and Shalom Harlow

Claudia Schiffer

Models Carolyn Murphy, Trish Goff, and Michele Hicks at Mark Eisen

Donna Karan Collection

SPRING/SUMMER
1997
CELEBRATING
THE FEMININE FORM

PRESENTED OCTOBER 1996

TRENDS:
TRANSPARENCY

THIS 1997 RUNWAY statement was covered but revealing. A more intellectual version of sex appeal was presented. This trend made retailers very nervous, as they felt they could not sell nude clothing. They breathed a sigh of relief when the clothes came in, and everything was lined.

Marc Jacobs

Ghost

RETURN OF THE SLIP

THIS SEASON'S SLIP was very different from Spring/Summer 1994's rock-and-roll version. The 1997 edition was elegant and dressed up Hollywood glamour style. Just weeks earlier, Carolyn Bessette had married John F. Kennedy, Jr. in what became the world's most famous slip dress overnight. Bessette's bridal gown was designed by Narciso Rodriguez.

VINTAGE

DESIGNERS DIPPED INTO
the past for inspiration from all decades.

Bob Mackie

Todd Oldham

Betsey Johnson's butterflies

Tall hair at Michael Kors

OTHER HIGHLIGHTS

Linda Evangelista's bob

Todd Oldham's denim

THE SCENE

★ General Motors commissioned Todd Oldham, Anna Sui, Nicole Miller, Richard Tyler, and Mark Eisen to design cars that were put on display at a party at the GM showroom on Fifth Avenue. Oldham's car was an Oldsmobile Bravada, which had hand-painted faux wood exterior and a plaid interior. Anna Sui's car was a GMC Yukon which was painted purple and had leopard-print carpeting. Each of the designer cars was auctioned and the profits went to the Nina Hyde Center for Breast Cancer Research. In addition, the designers were all given black versions of the car they designed.

★ Liz Claiborne celebrated its twentieth anniversary with a multimedia event that included a video retrospective, a runway show starring Niki Taylor, and a performance by Eartha Kitt.

★ American Express gave forty cardholders the chance to attend three shows, a cocktail party, and breakfast with several accessories designers. The cost of the package was $600.

★ Samsung provided free doughnuts to all attending the shows at the tents.

★ Elton John was hit in the face with a camera at the Versus show. John went backstage, and all was fine as he was unharmed.

★ Guests leaving the Versus show were approached by scalpers looking to buy their tickets to upcoming shows.

Liz Claiborne

Elton John

NARCISO RODRIGUEZ

Narciso Rodriguez became a household name in 1996, when his friend Carolyn Bessette wore his simple slip dress to marry John F. Kennedy, Jr. Rodriguez launched his line the following year. In 2005, he became the first American to win the CFDA Womenswear Designer of the Year award two years in a row. Rodriguez's designs have been worn by the likes of Michelle Obama, Kate Winslet, Claire Danes, Rachel Weisz, and Sarah Jessica Parker.

EILA MELL: Did you always want to be a designer?

NARCISO RODRIGUEZ: I have always wanted to be a designer. I love creating for women. The only other discipline I ever really considered was architecture.

EM: What is the main difference between showing your collection in New York and in Europe?

NR: New York is the most visible international platform for fashion and for designers. It is the reason so many designers come to show here, especially new ones. Having shown in Europe and in New York for many years I still believe that New York is the place where a designer can be most visible and not get lost on the fashion calendar.

EM: What do you love most about your job?

NR: The craft is what I love most. There are many aspects to a designer's work, but the part that I enjoy the most is evolving the craft from season to season.

EM: What would people be surprised to know about New York Fashion Week?

NR: The amount of work that goes into producing Fashion Week. The entire city feels mobilized to get things up and running and then taken apart, only to repeat it all in a few months.

FRESH FACES

KIARA KABUKURU

FROM: KAMPALA, UGANDA | HEIGHT: 5'8½"
HAIR: BROWN | EYES: BROWN

KYLIE BAX

FROM: THAMES, NEW ZEALAND | HEIGHT: 5'10"
HAIR: BLONDE | EYES: GREEN/GREY

MEGHAN DOUGLAS

Meghan Douglas got her start as a model by entering Elite's Look of the Year contest. She was one of the most popular models of the 1990s, appearing on the covers of *Harper's Bazaar*, *Elle*, *Cosmopolitan*, *Allure*, and many others.

EILA MELL: What was it like being part of the supermodel era?

MEGHAN DOUGLAS: Being part of the supermodel era was one of the most exciting and care-free stages in my life. The amazing part of it was working with extremely talented and creative people who could change a duckling like me into a swan.

EM: How have changes in your hair affected your career?

MD: I have had almost every hair color, but a red head has more fun! When Steven Meisel and his incredible team changed me into a redhead my career soared. His guidance and kindness I could never repay.

EM: Did you always want to be a model?

MD: As a young girl, I would see photos of Paulina Porizkova and I fell in love with fashion and photography. I never thought I was pretty. I dreamed of being a model and was lucky to have my dreams come true.

EM: Any favorite memories from Bryant Park?

MD: The fashion shows at Bryant Park were somewhere you would see so many friends all in one place, and laugh and cry about life.

EM: What would people be surprised to know about NY Fashion Week?

MD: That it's actually organized mayhem, even though it seems completely chaotic at times.

Cyndi Lauper and Cannon, celebrity stylist

Isaac Mizrahi

SNAPPED!

Susan Sarandon

Esther Cañadas

Oscar de la Renta

FALL/WINTER

1997

A TAILORED SEASON

PRESENTED APRIL 1997

TRENDS:
TAILORING

DESIGNERS TOOK AN interest in technique. Stella McCartney's influence at Chloe was felt, and for Fall/Winter 1997 Savile Row bespoke tailoring was unquestionably *in*.

Isaac Mizrahi

Carolina Herrera

BLACK

BACK TO BLACK; the fashion uniform that never goes away.

Halston, model: Rebecca Romijn

D, model: Angela Lindvall

MINIS

OTHER HIGHLIGHTS

Bangs at Todd Oldham

Halston's cutout

Isaac Mizrahi's lace

Dramatic eyes at Todd Oldham

THE SCENE

★ Donatella Versace's Versus show included a performance by the British band Republica.

★ Badgley Mischka had $8 million worth of Fred Leighton's jewelry in their show.

★ Jennifer Tilly jumped on Jill Stuart's runway for photographers. Rumor was her bag was stolen during the impromptu photo shoot.

★ There was big buzz surrounding the relaunch of Halston and newly appointed designer Randolph Duke. The show's backers went all out and hired many top models, including Linda Evangelista, Claudia Schiffer, and Helena Christensen. At first Evangelista wasn't interested in doing the show, as she was sitting out Fashion Week this season. However, Sandra Graham, Halston's Director of Public Relations and Advertising, cajoled her agent for weeks until she finally agreed. Evangelista was so taken with Randolph Duke that she told him not to bother sending a bill for the show.

Linda Evangelista

Badgley Mischka

Jennifer Tilly

DARYL KERRIGAN

Designer Daryl Kerrigan got her start doing wardrobe for films such as *My Cousin Vinny* and *Mystery Train*. Kerrigan started a line called Daryl K, and achieved great success with her low-slung pants.

EILA MELL: Although you've been on the fashion calendar, you've never actually showed your line, Daryl K, in Bryant Park. Is there any reason why?

DARYL KERRIGAN: It was because I was always looking for a venue that would speak about a feeling I wanted to convey. I wasn't able to get that across in the tents so I always showed offsite. I showed in a swimming pool in October on the Lower East Side. I had kind of a water thing going on. I showed in a bank. I also showed on the roof of the Lever Building. It's very beautiful. The garden where we showed had birds flying around. It was magnificent. You get all these added effects; the air, the sunlight, and the feeling of real life, which is what inspires me.

EM: What do you think defined you as a designer?

DK: I was about finding a new way of dressing women for the 1990s. It had a lot to do with a suit, but I reworked it. Everything was always stretch. It was a revolutionary way of looking at clothing—with sex appeal but also flattering the intellect. It was copied all over the world. I developed a stretch leather legging. If you had any feeling for rock and roll or downtown you had to have them. Paired with a beautifully tailored jacket, a silk shirt, and a fabulous bag, it's a completely understood look; then it was new.

EM: Your pants really were so successful. How did you develop them?

DK: I found a pair of men's pants in a vintage store. I fit them endlessly until I got the fit I wanted. That little bootleg—it wasn't flair and it wasn't straight. It was very particular. I think it made such an impact because there was nothing else like it out there.

FRESH FACES

TANGA MOREAU

FROM: BRUSSELS, BELGIUM | HEIGHT: 5' 8½" | HAIR: BLONDE | EYES: BLUE/GREEN

KAREN ELSON

FROM: MANCHESTER, ENGLAND
HEIGHT: 5'10" HAIR: RED | EYES: BLUE

ERIN O'CONNOR

FROM: WALSALL, ENGLAND | HEIGHT: 6'
HAIR: BROWN | EYES: HAZEL

ALEK WEK

FROM: WAU, SUDAN | HEIGHT: 5'11"
HAIR: BLACK | EYES: BROWN

RANDOLPH DUKE

Randolph Duke broke into fashion designing swimwear. In 1996 he famously designed the collection for the re-launch of the iconic Halston label. After leaving Halston, he showed at New York Fashion Week under his own name. Duke's designs have been on many red carpets. Hilary Swank and Marcia Gay Harden both won Academy Awards clad in Randolph Duke. He is also author of *The Look: A Guide to Dressing from the Inside Out.*

EILA MELL: How was showing as Randolph Duke different from showing as the designer for Halston?

RANDOLPH DUKE: With Halston I had a blissful ignorance about what was going on behind the scenes. A lot of people told me afterward they had been worried about what was going to happen to this iconic brand; how could someone try to recreate it? They were thinking the worst was going to happen. I remember Polly Mellen saying it was a disaster waiting to happen. You see, so many people had grown up with Halston. I became a designer because of Halston. He was a superstar designer. Those were really big shoes to fill.

The experience of that collection had kind of a magical quality. I had assembled a lot of the former employees of Halston—the tailors, seamstresses, patternmakers. In a spiritual sense, it had a life of its own. I learned so much from these people, who were with me trying to create something new and carry on his name. We bonded, and as a result we didn't pay too much attention to what was happening on the outside. We had a job to do and we created something special. I think the results were appreciated.

There's an atmosphere and energy, a moment that doesn't happen every time like that Halston moment. I think the biggest contribution was probably Linda Evangelista, and a simple thing like a smile that she cracked at the end of the runway. If the collection had been bad and she'd done that it wouldn't have made a difference. But there was something about that moment—from then on they were kind of with me.

I also remembered Linda preparing, doing a look session, and there was a level of professionalism about her that I had never experienced in a model before. I don't think she'd mind me saying this—she wore a dress in the finale of that first Halston show that was kind of sheer; it had a nude G-string that went under it. I always made my G-strings with no elastic in them, so you couldn't see any line. I was fanatical about that. And she put the dress on, and she said, "I . . . I have to shave." I just thought, "Well, that's—that's fucking awesome, that she's gonna go ahead and shave to wear my dress. I mean, I don't think anybody had ever given that level of commitment.

EM: How important is where you show the collection?

RD: All the ingredients have to come together—the clothes, the models, the space. Showing in Bryant Park offered convenience. They had a lot of amenities and knew how to do it like clockwork. The negative is that sometimes you can lose originality or a sense of thinking outside of the box that comes when you have to create an environment in an original space. It's a funny double-edged sword. Getting there is part of the experience. They may complain about driving uptown to a museum or going to the armory to see a Marc Jacobs show, but it's part of the experience. And it can set you apart.

EM: What are some of the things you remember from the Bryant Park years?

RD: There were times when I had to roll racks up the street from the studio and wear dark sunglasses and a hat so people wouldn't know it was me hauling a rack to my own show!

One time we were setting up late at night for a morning show the next day. I had ordered, I think it was gray carpeting and the carpet didn't arrive. So we didn't have a floor. Somebody went out and got some cheap carpeting and it looked cheap. It didn't work. Being an improviser, I had somebody go out and buy pounds of silver paillettes, and we sprinkled the entire runway with these silver sequins. It wasn't planned but it came out so beautiful. I think what you have to do as a designer is look at something and it either works or it doesn't. The mistake can almost work for you in a weird way. I think the sequined runway made the show in a way. It reflected all this light up into the models' skin. It was very dreamy and it was the right mood for the theme of the collection, which had a Greek goddess throwback feel to it.

I have fond memories of doing the shows at Bryant Park. There's kind of a ritual that sets in. I like ritual and routine, and I think I always felt that there was something I could depend on there; things would go smoothly. They had top-notch lighting and good technical execution. There are things people don't think about when they go to a fashion show. If the racks aren't high enough your clothes are dragging on the ground. If they don't sweep the floor at the venue then all the lint and thread from the previous show goes onto the hems of your dresses; under the spotlights of a show it's glaring—you see everything from the front row. One of the things they did well at Bryant Park was to mind those details. I know that sounds like kind of an unimportant detail, but I don't think people realize that's what goes on between each of the shows.

EM: Up to what point before the show are you still editing your collection?

RD: I wish longer! I never considered myself a great editor. And I think many times I could have used more editing. Sometimes less can be more. Once I rolled a show in that I don't think I ever edited anything out of. There were so many other things to concentrate on. Editing would have pushed me over the edge! There was one thing in that Halston show that, when I look at the tape, I always say, "Why?" And I know why I did it. I put that dress in because I decided to use my fit model in the show. Because of that I threw a dress in that didn't really work in the rotation. It was out-of-sync,

color wise. It just didn't work.

EM: How important is the choice of models to a show?

RD: I think a model is very important. We've had periods where supermodels really added something and brought glamour, excitement, and a wow factor to the shows. It seems to be different now. There's more of a mannequin quality to a lot of the girls. In a way I almost prefer that because, for me, it does bring a little bit more of the focus to the clothing.

EM: You have a special affection for Linda Evangelista.

RD: To me she was a model that had a beatific quality that I could never get other models to exude. I put that word up backstage in my instructions, and they'd all ask what it meant. I say to look like they'd just seen angels coming out of the clouds. It's a hard thing to instruct somebody to do. And she always had the ability to do that. I think not only in live situations but also in photographs.

EM: What's your favorite part of a fashion show?

RD: The very moment before it starts. It's at once a very nerve-wracking and heart-pounding moment. There is no going back. I think it's probably the moment of the whole process where you are so in the moment, you are so present, you can't be anywhere else. Once they're in the first looks there's really nothing to be racing around about, because until that model comes back the madness doesn't start again. There's nothing to do. We're ready to go. There's a moment of grace where you've created this and are now sending it out into the world. It's a beautiful moment.

EM: What is it like when you see someone in real life wearing your designs?

RD: It's always flattering in some regards, and it's always a little bit surprising too. You never really know who is buying your clothes, what type of women. It's often very diverse and it might be different than you expect. It's particularly wonderful when they recognize you and thank you for contributing to some aspect of their life. I've had a lot of women say they've never felt more beautiful, or that they met their husband wearing one of my dresses. Then I really feel like I've done my job. What I set out to do is to really help women feel beautiful.

Brandy

the Pit

SNAPPED!

Backstage at Betsey Johnson

Models at Richard Tyler

SPRING/SUMMER
1998
A CHANGE OF VENUE
PRESENTED NOVEMBER 1997

TRENDS:
CROPPED PANTS

SPRING/SUMMER 1998 was the season of the capri. The cropped pant was a huge trend and a key item for every mass retailer.

Bill Blass

Anna Sui

BEADING

DESIGNERS EMBRACED "bling," and heavily embellished their garments.

Michael Kors

COLOR

Marc Jacobs

Betsey Johnson, model: Ivanka Trump

THE SCENE

★ The biggest news this season was the change of venue from Bryant Park to the Chelsea Piers. Many attendees found the move to be disastrous. Suzy Menkes was quoted as saying it didn't smell like fashion. Others criticized the location as inconvenient—its remoteness, the lack of restaurants, navigating the West Side Highway, lack of taxis, people falling down the stairs, etc.

★ Spring 1998 marked the first season of shows after the tragic death of Gianni Versace. The fifty-year-old designer was returning home to his Miami Beach mansion when he was shot and killed by Andrew Cunanan. The fashion industry was shocked and deeply saddened by the loss of their beloved friend. Days later, Cunanan committed suicide.

★ Stephen Sprouse was back on the runway this season. Sprouse had licensing deals with the Andy Warhol Foundation and Staff International. The show was held at Staff's offices.

★ The Daryl K show was held in an empty pool this season. Designer Daryl Kerrigan's fascination with nature was incorporated into her collection. She had a print of a photograph of the inside of a body, which was painted onto her clothing.

Backstage at Carolina Herrera

Jodie Kidd

FRESH FACE

MAGGIE RIZER

FROM: STATEN ISLAND, NY | HEIGHT: 5'10" | HAIR: BLONDE | EYES: BLUE

"Marc Jacobs was my first show. I was scared to death that I was going to fall flat on my face. Marc and Robert very patiently helped talk me through walking in their heels. They kept saying, 'Try to look up. Try not to stumble.' They were very kind. Being forced to walk in heels has definitely turned out for the better!"

—Maggie Rizer

MAGGIE RIZER

Maggie Rizer's modeling career began when her mother sent her photo to Ford Models. She has been on the cover of numerous magazines, including *Vogue, George,* and *Vogue Italia.* In 1998 she was named VH1's Model of the Year. She has walked the runway for the leading fashion designers, as well as for Victoria's Secret. Rizer has appeared on *Sex and the City, Stylista,* and *America's Next Top Model.*

EILA MELL: What was the most unusual thing you've ever witnessed during Fashion Week?

MAGGIE RIZER: The PETA people can get a little rough, and photographers taking pictures of naked girls. There's a lack of boundaries sometimes.

EM: Do you ever get to keep any of the clothes you modeled in the shows?

MR: Some designers pay you in their clothes which is fantastic! My closet has a lot of Anna Sui and Marc Jacobs!

EM: Is it more fun to be in the show or to be in the audience?

MR: Being in the show for sure. Watching shows is very stressful with everyone pushing, trying to get the best seat, trying to be photographed. Being in a show is a breeze compared to that—and you get out of there faster.

EM: How is New York Fashion Week different from Fashion Weeks in other cities?

MR: I always preferred it because at the end of the day I could go home! It's nice after a long day constantly being the center of attention to be with friends in the comfort of your home.

EM: Is it a special honor to open or close a show?

MR: It's nice because you're representing the designer a bit more. At least you know they like you if you're first or last.

EM: Has a haircut or color ever affected your bookings?

MR: Everybody likes change, as long as it's a good change.

EM: What's your favorite part of NY Fashion Week?

MR: Seeing people you haven't seen in a while—and it being over!

EM: What would people be surprised to know about Fashion Week in New York?

MR: Backstage can actually be quite relaxing. You see everyone in one place and sometimes can even catch up on phone calls and emails.

SNAPPED!

Nicole Miller

FALL/WINTER

1998

RUNNING IN HEELS ...
BACK TO BRYANT PARK

PRESENTED APRIL 1998

TRENDS: LONG LENGTHS

THE LONG LENGTH of Fall 1998 was a reaction to the previous year's minis. There were sweeping lengths on everything from coats to skirts to dresses. It was a happy time for retailers, as more fabric means more money.

Patrick Robinson, model: Bridget Hall

Badgley Mischka

WINTER WHITE

DESIGNERS CHOSE TO break that old rule of not wearing white after Labor Day.

Michael Kors

Oscar de la Renta

FUR TRIM

FUR TRIM WAS on everything: jackets, hems of skirts, collars, etc. This was a great season for J. Mendel designer Gilles Mendel, who was innovative in his use of fur as fabric.

Cynthia Rowley's cup and saucer

Braids at Anna Sui, model: Audrey Marnay

OTHER HIGHLIGHTS

Beach Hair at Ralph Lauren, model: Esther Cañadas

Two-tone hair at Betsey Johnson

CUSTO DALMAU

In 1981, Custo Dalmau and his brother David started a T-shirt business. Almost thirty years later, that business, Custo Barcelona, is thriving, now also including everything from swimwear to coats.

EILA MELL: Is there one piece that Custo Barcelona is most known for?

CUSTO DALMAU: We started doing T-shirts in 1981, and that's our best-selling piece. On the runway you will not see T-shirts though because runway is an experimental opportunity to try new things, not the more commercial product. We have two lines. One is called Premium, which is the collection we show in New York. The other is Pure Custo, which is our basics.

EM: Who is your typical client?

CD: A person with a young spirit who understands fashion and is an individual.

EM: Would you ever do a more minimal collection?

CD: We did that and it was a complete failure. We delivered a very good product, but it was plain. People always associate a name with a product, and to them Custo Barcelona is graphic and colorful.

EM: What is Fashion Week like for you?

CD: It's a very focused exercise in trying to show the work of six months in fifteen minutes.

EM: How difficult is it to come up with something new every six months?

CD: It's difficult. You have to keep reinventing yourself.

EM: How important is the choice of models for a show?

CD: It's very important because to wear graphic and colors you have to feel comfortable. Not everybody can wear our collection. We choose the models who really feel good wearing the product, who embody the energy of the show. We also like to bring new faces to the runway as a way to stay fresh.

EM: What is the difference between designing for men and women?

CD: Women like to take risks. You have a lot of freedom. Designing for men is more difficult, especially when you work with colors and graphics.

EM: Do you feel the reaction to your clothing varies from country to country?

CD: Yes. We've found a relationship between color and sun. People from warm climates understand color. New York can be a tough city and color is almost taboo. In Florida, Los Angeles, and Hawaii it's the opposite; we sell out there.

EM: How do your accessories relate to your collections?

CD: We try to bring the same language to the accessories. Our DNA is fusion of graphics, colors, and materials.

EM: What's the most enjoyable part of Fashion Week?

CD: Organizing the show. It's a learning experience. You learn from the possibilities you create.

THE SCENE

★ The shows returned to Bryant Park after a one-season hiatus at Chelsea Piers. The move to the piers was caused by lack of available space in Bryant Park. It was also attributed to complaints such as lawn damage. Mayor Rudy Giuliani got involved and, along with Deputy Mayor Rudy Washington, got the shows back at Bryant Park. The event's organizers agreed to move the tents closer to Avenue of the Americas to satisfy Ark Restaurants, owners of the Bryant Park Grill. Ark previously complained that the restaurant's view was obscured by the tents.

★ General Motors signed on as the title sponsor, which led to the showing of the collections being called General Motors Fashion Week. GM saw this as a way to target female customers.

★ Giorgio Armani brought his show to New York after Paris police shut his Emporio Armani show down citing security reasons. The Armani show took place at Cipriani Wall Street.

★ Gwen Stefani attended Donatella Versace's Versus show. It was the superstar singer's first appearance at Fashion Week.

★ Donald Trump was unable to get into the Halston show. As a consolation he attended the after party, where he met model Melania Knauss, his future wife.

Giorgio Armani

BERI SMITHER

International cover girl and American model Beri Smither has strutted and posed for the top names in the fashion industry, including Chanel, Donna Karan, Armani, Versace, Krizia, Oscar de la Renta, and Prada, and she has graced the covers of *Allure*, *Cosmopolitan*, *British Vogue*, *Elle*, *Marie Claire*, and *Glamour*. She has worked with famous photographers such as Herb Ritts, Patrick Demarchelier, Steven Meisel, and Bruce Weber, to name a few. Beri was also featured in the 1998 *Sports Illustrated* Swimsuit Issue. After more than fifteen years of modeling, she is still making her mark in the industry as a model and talent/model manager.

EILA MELL: What's the most fun part of NY Fashion Week?

BERI SMITHER: Getting to wear amazing clothes; having the fashion community from all over the world in New York for that week; connecting and working with the best editors; going to dinner parties; seeing old and new friends.

EM: Any favorite memories from the tents?

BS: Seeing amazingly gorgeous women sleeping on the floor of a tent just moments away from sashaying in sheer elegance down the runway.

EM: What would people be surprised to know about NY Fashion Week?

BS: The exclusivity factor when booking a model. Sometimes clients don't want models to do multiple shows so they won't book you if you're doing another show the same day. For example, when Prada books a model exclusively, the model is only allowed to walk one runway—Prada. Or if Calvin Klein books a model on an exclusive basis for Tuesday, he/she is not allowed to do any other show that day. Sometimes models will be hired exclusively by one designer for the whole season or exclusively to one city in order to avoid any delays or challenges that could occur in the model's schedule.

FRESH
FACE

ANN-CATHERINE LACROIX

FROM: BRUSSELS, BELGIUM | HEIGHT: 5'10" | HAIR: BLONDE | EYES: BLUE

Kathleen Turner

Christina Ricci

Patti LaBelle

SNAPPED!

Todd Oldham

Liz Tilberis

Maggie Rizer

Carolina Herrera

SPRING/SUMMER
1999
CHANGING THE FASHION CALENDAR

PRESENTED SEPTEMBER 1998

TRENDS:
TURTLENECKS

ALTHOUGH NOT A typical spring/summer item, turtlenecks showed up on a number of runways.

Ralph Lauren

Michael Kors

CARGO PANTS

THIS SEASON CARGO pants went from the campus to the runways. Designers' grown-up versions (in luxe fabrics) could take consumers from the office to a night on the town.

PASTELS

A SWEET CONFECTION of spring-like hues shown on the runway.

Marc Jacobs

DKNY

"No makeup" makeup at Joan Vass, model: Adriana Lima

OTHER HIGHLIGHTS

Hair at Michael Kors

DKNY

THE SCENE

★ Ten New York designers, including Helmut Lang, Nicole Miller, Calvin Klein, and Donna Karan, made a bold statement by moving up their shows to make them the first stop, rather than the last, on the fashion calendar.

★ Absent from Fashion Week this season was DKNY head designer Jane Chung. Chung was on maternity leave.

Helmut Lang

Gwyneth Paltrow holding up a sign with her name, in case the press didn't know who she was

Gwyneth Paltrow

FRESH FACES

SYLVIA VAN DER KLOOSTER

FROM: AMSTERDAM, THE NETHERLANDS
HEIGHT: 5'10" | HAIR: BROWN
EYES: GREEN

COLETTE PECHEKHONOVA

FROM: SAINT PETERSBURG, RUSSIA
HEIGHT: 5'10½" | HAIR: BLONDE | EYES: BLUE

JAMES AGUIAR

James Aguiar got his start in fashion as fashion director at Bergdorf Goodman. He was a host of the Emmy-nominated television series *Full Frontal Fashion*, as well as *Style Court, Behind the Label,* and *Where D'Ya Get That?* Aguiar is a contributor for the website FirstComesFashion.com, which live streams shows from New York Fashion Week.

EILA MELL: What did you think of the move to Lincoln Center?

JAMES AGUIAR: I thought it was phenomenal. It was really well organized. It's like an airport! It looked great. The space was also able to accommodate presentations for smaller designers who didn't do runway shows. You get to see the clothes close up. And I got the first interview with Fern Mallis for FirstComes Fashion.com.

EM: I think the website is great. You had so many shows.

JA: We got permission to stream about thirty-five shows.

EM: What's the concept behind it?

JA: It's really taking the velvet rope off the shows and being able to see them live. We all get this information almost immediately. We stream the arrivals live, the front of the house, and then the actual show. I think it's great for fashion addicts, trend spotters, and people in the industry. We have personalities—Judy Licht, Robert Verdi, Christina Ha, Constance White, and myself—so many people who have been in the industry in many different aspects. We do the wrap up, talk to designers, and have fun.

EM: When did you start going to NY Fashion Week?

JA: Probably around 1994.

EM: Were you there at the very beginning of the tents in Bryant Park?

JA: Yes, but I was sneaking in for standing-room placement. I remember the circus aspect of it. There wasn't as much media coverage back then. But I remember certain people being interviewed and I thought, "I wonder what you have to do to be interviewed." Then I became the fashion director for Bergdorf's and I was the person being interviewed. Then I thought, "I'd really like to be the person doing the interviewing!" Next I got my job at *Full Frontal Fashion*, so I was doing that.

EM: How did you make that happen?

JA: When I left Bergdorf's I went to Paris to work for Nina Ricci. When I got back I got a phone call from the executive producer of *Full Frontal*. She asked me if I wanted to replace Robert Verdi. I was very happy—great gig!

EM: What are some of the more unusual things you've seen during Fashion Week?

JA: Early on there were times it was like a club environment. There were velvet ropes, people were yelling and screaming and pushing and clamoring to get in. Alexander McQueen showed in a synagogue on the Lower East Side. It's where Sarah Jessica Parker got married. That scene was such a madhouse. People were screaming. Then Anna Wintour showed up, but nobody was getting into the show. People were yelling, "You have to let this woman in." It was like a punk rock concert. She was airlifted and bodysurfed over the crowd into the show.

EM: What are the politics involved in front-row seating?

JA: The front row is editors, retailers, celebrities, friends of the designer—and crashers. The truth is the PR people hold a lot of front-row seats because they never know who's going to show up. I guarantee you even at Michael Kors or Marc Jacobs you can snag a front-row seat if you're smart.

EM: So, would you rather be in the back row at a show or not at all? Is it not good to be seen in the back?

JA: No. I've seen André Leon Talley in the third row. I think at a certain point, when you've seen as many shows as we have, that sort of goes away. I think the quest for the front row is a very shallow pursuit. It's nice when you have a front-row seat. You can see the clothes better, and there is definitely a caché to that. But I've been in the front. I've been in the back. I've been in the middle. I've been outside! For me it doesn't really matter, though it does for a lot of people.

EM: Any favorite shows?

JA: I never want to miss Michael Kors, Narciso Rodriguez, Oscar de la Renta, or Carolina Herrera. These are the stalwarts of the industry. I also love the Blonds. I used to love the Heatherette shows, too.

EM: Richie Rich and the Blonds are such hot tickets.

JA: It's a club-kid crowd. But these are also designers that have dressed everybody from Rihanna to Beyoncé, Fergie, and Katy Perry. They're tuned in to pop culture.

EM: So they're not going to get the Oscar de la Renta crowd?

JA: Probably not. Although I wish they would. When I was at Bergdorf's I was always looking around the corner for somebody different. I think that's what we should be doing. When I see a bunch of club kids with the Blonds I feel like the mainstream media or editor of a magazine should take a responsibility in covering that, because these are the people that are shaping the way young girls look at celebrity.

EM: Are there some people that cover both kinds of shows?

JA: Sally Singer's a brave editor, and the people at *Paper*.

EM: Which new designers do you think are exciting?

JA: There's a new girl, Sally LaPointe, whose show was phenomenal. She presented a head-to-toe, fully realized vision right out of the gate. We tend to give a lot of glory to young designers, I feel, before their time. So to see somebody that does have real talent and is thinking outside of the box is great. But I was very disappointed there wasn't a bigger crowd to witness that.

EM: Fashion has really emerged into the mainstream over the past ten years or so.

JA: There's always been a fascination with fashion. Now you see stylists getting famous for working with celebrities. You see designers getting reality shows. *Project Runway* gives the winner $100,000, which seems like a lot of money. That's what it would take to show, and that's just to mount the production with lights, dressers, the stage, invitations, and hair and makeup. Then you have to factor in the clothes, and the fact that if those clothes don't sell, you've already got to be designing the next pieces.

But I think that shows like *Project Runway* and *The Rachel Zoe Project*, and the movie *The Devil Wears Prada* are fantastic—anything that can glamorize and bring more people into the industry is great. Now everybody wants to be a stylist though. What I always tell them is, "You will be schlepping clothes. That's what you do—even if you aspire to be a celebrity stylist. Sometimes people don't really understand what it's really like because they see the glamorous side.

EM: How does your retail background help you as an interviewer?

JA: I feel it gives me a great advantage to know designers from a retail standpoint because I'm able to ask more informed questions, which I think puts them at ease. It's not just about celebrities or what the colors are or what their inspiration is. Asking the right questions will bring out what the inspiration is. Being a good fashion reporter is not about holding a microphone and asking bland questions. It's about knowledge of fashion history, the industry as a whole, and costume design.

It's about understanding that nothing's really new and being able to reference things. This gets the best out of a designer and puts a celebrity at ease.

EM: Who was your first interview with?

JA: Kimora Lee Simmons. She had a show called *Life & Style* that I was on. I was waiting to interview her. There was always a mob scene around her. She pulled me in and screamed at me, "I see you got a real job!" I liked that.

EM: Who is another favorite interviewee?

JA: Karl Lagerfeld. After I interviewed him I thought, "Wow. That was a milestone." He's very intimidating, but he's very nice—he's surrounded by tons of press though. To watch him go from English to German to French to Italian, and be able to tell a joke in all of these languages is shocking. His knowledge is so immense and intimidating. And Anna Wintour was a favorite, of course. You have to be on your game interviewing her.

EM: What's something you love about the industry?

JA: It's all based on perfect presentation on the runway—then to be able to glimpse behind the scenes where models are sleeping or drunk or ripping off their clothes, or doing hair and makeup and running to the next show. I love that duality, the peek behind the curtain.

EM: What would people be surprised to know about NY Fashion Week?

JA: A show is exciting and fun, but it's only eleven minutes. The most shocking thing is how organized and sane and controlled it actually is. It's a seamless operation. And really, at the end of the day, it's a trade show. A very glamorous trade show.

James Aguiar with the Heatherette boys, Traver Rains and Richie Rich

Tinsley Mortimer and Aguiar

Vivienne Tam

FALL/WINTER

1999

GETTING READY
FOR THE YEAR 2000

PRESENTED APRIL 1999

TRENDS:
SPACE AGE

THE SPAGE-AGE trend seen on the runways for Fall/Winter 1999 was a reaction to the approaching millennium. Designers were expected to create clothes for the future.

Anna Sui, model: Carmen Kass

Oscar de la Renta, model: Esther Cañadas

BALL
GOWNS

RED CARPET DRESSING hit its height as designers, many of whom made their name on the red carpet, brought the same looks to the runways.

CHUNKY KNITS

WITH Y2K ON the horizon, the idea of burying yourself in your clothes became more attractive. Fabrics were luxurious, giving a feeling of security, nesting, and insulation.

Oscar de la Renta

Marc Jacobs

OTHER HIGHLIGHTS

Philip Treacy's hats

Middle parts at Donald Deal, model: Melania Knauss

Makeup at Vivienne Westwood

THE SCENE

- ★ A five-months pregnant Cindy Crawford walked the runway for Ellen Tracy.

- ★ Bill Blass announced his plan to retire in 2000.

- ★ The invitation to Helmut Lang's show asked his audience to come in black-tie attire.

- ★ Sugar Ray performed at Tommy Hilfiger's show at Roseland.

- ★ Menswear shows no longer had their own Fashion Week due to the New York shows, now scheduled before Europe's Fashion Weeks. The men's shows began sharing the week with the women's.

- ★ Special appearance: Alan Cumming at Cynthia Rowley

Alan Cumming at Cynthia Rowley

Cindy Crawford

WARIS DIRIE

Waris Dirie was born in the region of Galcaio near the border of Ethiopia. At the age of thirteen she fled to London to escape a forced marriage to a sixty-one-year-old man. Her modeling career was born when she was discovered by photographer Terence Donovan. Dirie was appointed as a UN Special Ambassador for the elimination of Female Genital Mutilation by the Secretary-General of the United Nations, Kofi Annan. In 1997 Waris Dirie's autobiography, *Desert Flower*, was published and became an international bestseller. A film version was released in 2009 with model Liya Kebede playing Dirie.

EILA MELL: How did you get involved in modeling?

WARIS DIRIE: I was approached by a photographer while leaving a YMCA in London. He asked if he could take my picture and I said yes. This is how I started modeling.

EM: What was your first job as a model?

WD: My first job was a shoot for an American magazine. I was standing on Coca-Cola cans. The photographer was David LaChapelle.

EM: What was your first season at Bryant Park like?

WD: I came to New York Fashion Week for the first time in 1995. It blew my mind. I felt like I was in the middle of a circus and I loved it.

EM: Is it more fun to be in the show or in the audience?

WD: In the show! While you're on the catwalk, you become someone else and you just put everything you have into those three minutes. This is your moment to shine!

EM: Can you tell me about your incredible work as a human rights activist?

WD: After writing my autobiographic novel, *Desert Flower*, the issue of female genital mutilation (FGM) received a lot of attention. I became a UN ambassador against FGM and gave countless speeches and interviews on the issue. In 2002, I started my own organization, the Waris Dirie Foundation, in Vienna. The foundation provides information and raises awareness on FGM, develops campaigns and projects, and supports victims and those threatened by FGM.

EM: You were also a Bond Girl. What was it like working on the film *The Living Daylights*?

WD: It was great. I mean, I got to rub oil on James Bond!

FRESH FACES

ISABELI FONTANA

FROM: CURITIBA, BRAZIL | HEIGHT: 5' 9½"
HAIR: BROWN | EYES: BLUE

YFKE STURM

FROM: ALMERE, THE NETHERLANDS
HEIGHT: 5'11" | HAIR: BLONDE
EYES: BLUE

MARY ALICE STEPHENSON

Mary Alice Stephenson is one of the world's most sought-after beauty and style experts. Her television credits include *The Oprah Winfrey Show, Good Morning America, Entertainment Tonight,* and *America's Most Smartest Model* (as co-host). Stephenson has also been both a fashion director and editor at magazines such as *Harper's Bazaar, Vogue,* and *Marie Claire.* Most importantly, she is the fashion wish ambassador for the Make-a-Wish Foundation.

EILA MELL: How does Fashion Week influence your work as a fashion editor and curator?

MARY ALICE STEPHENSON: I try to weed through and convey to my following what I feel they really need to know to make their lives easier. You take this; you bring life to it; you tell a story with it. You put fashion into the work culturally, putting your own magazine's version into something relevant that people can connect with.

EM: How has New York Fashion Week changed during the Bryant Park years?

MAS: There used to be exclusivity. There were no live broadcasts; people didn't have cameras. The show was that moment where the designer's vision was revealed. All the information that was gathered was utilized to arrive at a magazine's point of view. We had the next few months to plan how to relay every fashion and beauty statement to the reader.

EM: Bloggers have certainly been a presence at recent shows. What's your take on that?

MAS: I think there is a place for that. There are certain people that followers connect with. The new users do not necessarily want to be dictated to. They don't need to keep up with the Joneses. It's the opposite now; people want to have their own personal style.

EM: Are trends important?

MAS: Yes. When it is important for a person to make a statement and represent themselves, they want to know all the options. For most people a sense of style is not innate. Trends help most people decide what is important to them. They need permission to break the rules and have fun with fashion. They need to be guided and they appreciate that. Women now more than ever are saying okay to trends at age forty, fifty, seventy. Blandness as women move up in years is not going to work anymore.

EM: Are there any rules for dressing anymore?

MAS: The only rule is to break the rule. You should dress for yourself. You can mix prints, wear denim with sequins. It is an exciting time to be a woman. There are so many options and you have to find what is right for you.

EM: How is fashion relevant to the average person?

MAS: Even when times are tough glamour helps keep sparkle in the world. There are so many things in the world you can't control; it feels good to control how you look. I have traveled the world and met many women who have suffered terrible things—cancer, the loss of their husbands; after going through so many difficulties, fashion is a relief. For the past ten years I have been with the Make-a-Wish Foundation. We cannot keep up with the requests to attend Fashion Week. Kids from all walks of life want to sit in the front row. That is their one wish. The brilliance, the beauty, the magic that is created; the art that comes out of that week is rare and special and needed. Fashion is a great healer.

MICHAEL MUSTO

New York nightlife fixture Michael Musto is best known for his long-running column in the *Village Voice*, "La Dolce Musto." He is frequently on television, with credits such as *The Daily Show with Jon Stewart*, *Countdown with Keith Olbermann*, and *Behind the Music*. Musto is author of the books *Downtown-V285*, *Manhattan on the Rocks*, and *La Dolce Musto: Writings by the World's Most Outrageous Columnist.*

EILA MELL: So is it true that you've often been mistaken for Isaac Mizrahi?

MICHAEL MUSTO: Yes! That's something that's happened through the years. And I'm always thrilled, because he's younger than I am—a little better looking too! I also get Al Franken.

EM: Is there a designer whose show you never miss?

MM: There's always one go-to show for the kind of downtown scene that I cover. It used to be Todd Oldham and Isaac. Then it became Heatherette, and now for me it's the Blonds. They attract a circus-y mixture of transsexuals and celebrities. You never know who'll be there, from Katy Perry to someone from *American Idol*—Adam Lambert's been there. Even if the fashions weren't good (which they are!) it would still be worth going to for the scene.

EM: Any favorite memories from the tents?

MM: One of the funnier things I've seen was at a Russell Simmons show. A model was walking down the runway and her drop earring fell off. And Russell Simmons, from across the runway, was motioning for me to pick it up! I just sat there stubbornly like, "I don't work for you!"

There was one year Marc Jacobs gave out a really expensive watch in his gift bag. Those were the glory days. Those days are over. Now you're lucky if you get a CD or a T-shirt—maybe some skin cream.

The old Isaac and Todd Oldham shows were so much fun. They were the places to be. It was always fun to see which of the three was going to be walking—Naomi Campbell, Christy Turlington, or Linda Evangelista. And

there was also tension. The word was out that Naomi hated Tyra Banks, and wouldn't model in a show where Tyra was modeling. So there was always that feeling, like what if somebody booked them both or something.

EM: What was the mood like after September 11?

MM: I think it was the night before September 11 that Marc Jacobs had a huge show. It was really hot. I remember people came out with bottles of water for certain VIPs like Anna Wintour. That made other people angry—that only selected people were being handed bottles of water. It was pretty much the height of extravagance and craziness. Marc's show was late. It was a frantic, urgent sit-around-and-wait kind of feeling, and it was exciting. One thing about Fashion Week is that so much of it is about status. It's not just about the clothing, but "Did I get invited?" "Did I get the front row?" "Did I get the after party invite?"

After September 11 people wanted to scale down. The mood of the country was not about indulging in outlandishly expensive outfits. A lot of people were doing showroom presentations instead of actual fashion shows.

EM: Was it big news around the tents when Robert Altman was shooting the film *Ready-to-Wear*?

MM: He was such a revered American director. Everyone was excited about the prospect of him doing a movie about fashion. I think Isaac has a part in it. A lot of designers got involved. It just seemed like a can't-fail project. I remember the premiere where people were just horrified. Isaac looked like he was going to vomit. I didn't think it was that bad, but I was definitely in the minority.

Oscar de la Renta,
model: Naomi Campbell

SPRING/SUMMER

2000

DENIM EVERYWHERE

PRESENTED SEPTEMBER 1999

TRENDS: PRINTS

PRINTS WERE ALL over the place for Spring/Summer 2000, from madcap to expected florals.

Tommy Hilfiger, model: Alek Wek

Vivienne Tam, model: Trish Goff

DENIM

FROM MARC JACOBS' colorful denim to Oscar de la Renta's double-faced denim evening gown, this was a huge trend for the season.

Betsey Johnson

Jill Stuart

FREE SPIRIT

WITH THE 1990S behind them, designers embraced the endless possibilities of the future.

Tiny clothes on Kate Moss for Versus

Bare midriffs at Randolph Duke, model: Heidi Klum

OTHER HIGHLIGHTS

Oscar de la Renta's necklace

Wind-blown hair at Daryl K

Tommy Hilfiger's boots

THE SCENE

Bill Blass's farewell show was scheduled on the same day that Hurricane Floyd hit New York. Blass agreed to cancel the show due to the terrible weather conditions, but Fern Mallis insisted they go forward. Mallis, wearing a rain coat and hat, informed the crowd gathered to see his final collection that the show was running late because of the weather, and to please be patient; that they could not let Mr. Blass leave without a proper goodbye. No one abandoned his show. At the conclusion, Blass received a standing ovation from the rapturous crowd. There was not a dry eye in the house. The tents were shut down after the show for the rest of the day.

Also contending with the hurricane was Alexander McQueen. His show was at Pier 94 on the West Side Highway. Instead of a runway, McQueen had his models walk through a shallow pool in the rain.

Glamour magazine had a reporter at the tents ask fashion insiders their opinion on a handbag. After giving their answers they were told that the bag's designer was Monica Lewinsky.

Anna Wintour took on one of Lisa Marie Presley's bodyguards at the Marc Jacobs show. Reportedly, the bodyguard grabbed Wintour by the arm and shoved her. Wintour pushed back, and made her way backstage to see Jacobs.

Chelsea Clinton was thanked in the program for the Marc Jacobs show. Jacobs president Robert Duffy said that they always get calls about the people in the program, and that they thought it would be funny to put Clinton's name in.

Betsey Johnson used non-models in her show, which was held in her showroom. The participants included her daughter Lulu, Amy Sacco, Lauren Ezersky, Amanda Lepore, Veruschka, and Johnson's yoga instructor. Instead of using a stylist, Johnson let each model prepare herself for the runway.

Boy George spun live for DKNY. The show celebrated the brand's first ten years, the first New York store, the first fragrance, and the first season of the millennium. After the show the crowd made its way to the after party at Donna Karan's store on 59th Street.

Tommy Hilfiger's show was part rock concert. Bush played to the crowd gathered at Madison Square Garden.

Bill Blass

Alexander McQueen

Patricia Field and Rebecca Weinberg modeling for Betsey Johnson

EMILY SANDBERG

Emily Sandberg has modeled for everyone from Dolce & Gabbana to Fendi to Calvin Klein. She is also an actress, and has appeared in the films *The Devil Wears Prada* and *Employee of the Month*.

EILA MELL: How did you get involved in modeling?

EMILY SANDBERG: My mom and grand-mother entered me in a modeling contest. I then joined Agency Models and Talent in Minneapolis and moved to New York six months later to join Next Models.

EM: What was your first job as a model?

ES: I did a lot of tests for free in New York at the beginning to build my book. The first job I got paid for was Macy's. I think I got $800 for a half day. Needless to say I was very excited and my agent was proud of me. I called my dad from the studio and thought it was so cool to be able to make long distance calls while at work.

EM: What was your first season at Bryant Park like?

ES: My first big show was Anna Sui. The energy back-stage was great. Anna's team always does a fantastic job organizing and keeping the flow moving. I'd never seen so many people in such small spaces. The tents felt like a maze, there were photographers outside taking photos of the models as they walked in. By the end of the week it felt like home away from home. I'd jump in a cab, zip up Sixth Avenue, and look forward to seeing all the makeup artists, hairstylists, designers, and everyone involved in the shows backstage. I really enjoyed the whole experience.

EM: What was the most unusual thing you've ever witnessed at New York Fashion Week?

ES: At one huge show which will remain nameless, all the heels kept breaking on the runway so backstage it got a little crazy trying to find heels to fit the models. Shoes were getting passed around and strapped on very quickly.

EM: Can you tell me about the NYC 2000 show?

ES: That was a lot of fun. I remember walking down the runway in Times Square feeling very confident. There was a ramp that slanted downward and doing the runway walk in heels back up it was difficult. Back-stage everyone was very excited and professional. My mom and grandma were able to be there. It was extra special for them to see me walk a runway in Times Square and have it broadcast on a huge screen.

EM: Has a haircut or color ever affected your bookings?

ES: My hair has been many different colors and lengths. Luigi Murenu cut my hair into a Mia Farrow pixie for a *Vogue Italia* cover story with Steven Meisel. I loved it and kept it that length for a season.

EM: How is NY Fashion Week different than Fashion Weeks in other cities?

ES: The nice thing about New York is I can go home at the end of the day to rest. It's comforting to be sur-rounded by familiarity at the end of a busy and long work day.

EM: What's your favorite part of NY Fashion Week?

ES: I love the drive and the passion that goes into the work. I love being in designers' showrooms at midnight. I love getting to see everyone pushing past the point of exhaustion to finish the collection. There's something very dramatic and also intimate that takes place when everyone from agents to designers to models are all pushing for the same goal.

EM: Do you have a favorite designer?

ES: I have a few in New York that I'm loyal to because they showed me loyalty in a business that switches models every few season—Marc Jacobs, Anna Sui, Donna Karan, Michael Kors, and Tuleh.

EM: What would people be surprised to know about NY Fashion Week?

ES: I was surprised to find out how small and intimate most of the shows are. I didn't realize that the spaces for the shows aren't huge, and that creates an air of exclusivity. I was also surprised to find out how kind and accommodating most of the people working on the shows are. It certainly wasn't the nose-in-the-air attitude I expected.

FRESH FACES

LIYA KEBEDE

FROM: ADDIS ABABA, ETHIOPIA | HEIGHT: 5'10"
HAIR: BROWN | EYES: BROWN

CAROLINE RIBEIRO

FROM: BELÉM DO PARÁ, BRAZIL | HEIGHT: 5'11" | HAIR: BLACK | EYES: BROWN

ANASTASIA KHOZZISOVA

FROM: SARATOV, RUSSIA | HEIGHT: 5'10" HAIR: BLONDE | EYES: GREEN

Linda Wells

Elsa Klensch

Vera Wang

SNAPPED!

Donatella Versace with Madonna in the audience (far left)

Dick Page and Gisele Bündchen

Halston

FALL/WINTER
2000
A LUXURIOUS SEASON
PRESENTED FEBRUARY 2000

TRENDS:
LUXURY

AMERICANS WERE SPENDING a lot on labels. Designers were now celebrities. This harkened back to the excess of the late 1980s, when luxury ruled the runways.

Michael Kors

Calvin Klein Collection, model: Carmen Kass

LONG COATS

FALL/WINTER 2000 saw a stream of sweeping, luxurious, expensive coats.

Calvin Klein Collection, model: Gisele Bündchen

Nicole Miller, model: Alek Wek

EVENING TROUSERS

GONE WERE BALL skirts; these trousers were the new way to dress for evening.

OTHER HIGHLIGHTS

Stephanie Seymour at Helmut Lang

Michael Kors glamour

NEW ON THE SCENE

SEAN JOHN

"The first Sean John show was spectacular. I think he took everybody by surprise. It was a beautiful production. There were expansive runways with airport runway lights running along the sides. There was a huge wall projecting images that were just moving fast and furious, and great music, which you can imagine. And he had the sexiest male models in the world! They all came down wearing great pastel colors and furs and they had diamond necklaces and diamond bracelets and every one of them looked more macho than the last one. I think everyone's jaw dropped and they thought, 'Oh my God!'"

—Fern Mallis

SNAPPED!

Chloe Sevigny

Cynthia Rowley

FRESH FACE

NICOLA BREYTENBACH

FROM: SOUTH AFRICA | HEIGHT: 5' 9½" | HAIR: BLONDE
EYES: GREEN

THE SCENE

★ PETA was out in full force this season. Michael Kors was hit in the face with a tofu cream pie while taking his curtain call. Oscar de la Renta's runway was stormed by two of the organization's members who held up signs and chanted "Oscar de la Renta: Fur pimp." But the biggest commotion was at Randolph Duke's show. During the show PETA member Brice Friedrich attempted to throw red paint on a model wearing fur. He was grabbed by security, and so instead of the model being doused, the paint splattered members of the audience, including Elsa Klensch and Phillip Bloch.

★ In a fax to *Women's Wear Daily*, Geoffrey Beene announced that his Fall 2000 show would be his final one. Beene later said he was bored with traditional runway shows, and was more interested in exploring other means of presenting his collections, such as the Internet, television, film, etc.

★ Donna Haag treated members of her audience to a unique experience at her show. The designer had videos of models on screens amid a maze of ice sculptures through which guests navigated. At the end was a room full of trees covered in snow with a number of Haag's dresses floating above the ground.

★ Designer Stephen Slowik was chosen to take the reins of the collection of the retired Bill Blass. Although Blass chose to step down, he remained active in the company as a consultant.

★ Photographers were unhappy at Donna Karan's show. The problem was that there was simply not enough space to accommodate all the invited cameramen, with more than fifty of them turned away. Although Karan's staff tried to find room for everyone, it was simply not possible. As a show of solidarity, the photographers who made it in left and boycotted the show, leaving only the house photographers and videographers to record the event.

In addition, eighteen people on their way to the Donna Karan show got stuck in an elevator for more than an hour.

If the elevator incident was not enough trouble for a single show, towards the end a fuse blew which left the Donna Karan models walking down the runway without music.

★ Gisele Bündchen was all set to walk the runway for Helmut Lang. The leading model of the day was fitted for several outfits, but Lang changed his mind at the last minute. He was reportedly concerned that Bündchen would overshadow the clothing and decided she should only appear to model a single look. Bündchen opted not to appear in the show at all and left.

★ Three weeks before Lola Faturoti was scheduled to show her Fall 2000 collection she learned that she had lost her funding. Unable to raise sufficient funding for a show, the designer took her rent money and created a thirteen-look collection. She had models wear her dresses outside of Ralph Lauren's show, although the designer was unaware of Faturoti's plans. The stunt paid off. Faturoti's guerilla fashion show got the attention of fashion insiders and was written about in the media.

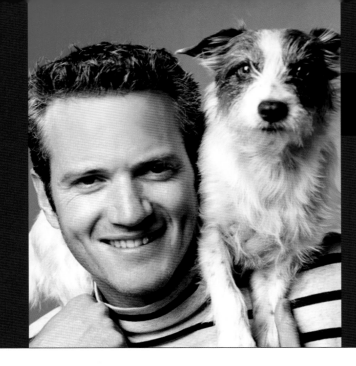

DAN MATHEWS

For more than twenty-five years Dan Mathews has been working with PETA (People for the Ethical Treatment of Animals). Mathews is the author of *Committed: A Rabble-Rouser's Memoir.*

EILA MELL: How did PETA start organizing protests at Bryant Park?

DAN MATHEWS: I've been with PETA since 1985. Back then our whole fur campaign was about going to protest outside a department store, trying to fight for legislation to ban the leg hold trap in one state. It was all very piecemeal. I started organizing the fur campaign in the late 1980s. In the '90s it seemed to me that the obvious ground zero for the whole fur issue was Bryant Park, where the designers are showing the stuff. Trying to embarrass them on their own turf seemed to be the way to go. We looked at a list of designers and sent nice letters to all of them and of course every single letter was ignored. We did a few protests. We did an occupation in Calvin Klein's office which resulted in him banning fur. Now Calvin and I are quite friendly. The best way was for them to really be wondering where we were going to show up uninvited. We had all these different people who would somehow get in and take over the runway when models wearing fur or designers who had fur were showing.

EM: What's it like taking over a runway?

DM: It's very nerve wracking, I've got to tell you. The fashion editors know you by face, so you always need new people to do it. I actually dressed as a priest and got into one show. I had a sign saying, "Thou Shalt Not Kill." We always try to give people a little bit of style. Sometimes we have people with nothing on, like in our "I'd Rather Go Naked Than Wear Fur" signs. Sandra Bernhard wrote in the *New Yorker* that the PETA protests are the sexiest thing about Fashion Week because it's the

only thing that was unpredictable; that it added edge and had kind of a rock ethic to it. We don't do it with the idea that the designers will have a change of heart. The impact is that the whole world hears about it.

EM: Why do you think so many designers use fur?

DM: Sometimes the furriers will give the designers a sponsorship if they use fur in the collections, even if it's not available for retail.

EM: What are some of the practices with which you take issue?

DM: To cut costs they now import from China, where they have no animal-protection laws. We have seen animals routinely being skinned alive. They're slammed into the ground by their hind legs. They're nailed to a post and skinned while their eyes are still fluttering. It's hideous, but designers will import the fur from China and not think too much of it because it's the cheapest option.

In the leather trade for instance, a lot of the cheapest leather comes from India. It's ironic because cows are sacred there, but there are a few states that allow cows to be killed. These cows are so feeble in their last weeks that they're falling down, and their tails are broken to get them off the ground. The furriers don't want to spend money to feed them; they rub chili peppers in the animals' eyes to keep them going. All this has been documented. It's cheaper, so that's why everyone was using leather from India.

Wool from Australia has a special cruelty that comes attached to it. Sheep are not native to Australia. Merino sheep are native to Spain. The sheep were genetically manipulated to make the animals have more and more skin, and therefore more wool that they could make more money from. What they didn't count on was the skin getting so dense that the animals couldn't even shit anymore—so they chop off all the skin around millions of lambs' backsides every year with no painkiller. That is now a common practice in Australia unique to that country.

We want people to please have some responsibility and not just use the cheapest option available, because usually animals have suffered as a result.

EM: Do you think PETA has made a difference in the fashion industry?

DM: Definitely. There are designers, such as Marc Bouwer, who used to use fur, leather, wool, etc. He heard about us through our protests and investigated what happens to the animals in these industries. Just on his own he decided to stop using fur and leather. He's still a credible, high-end designer. Ralph Lauren stopped using fur altogether. Calvin Klein asked me if I ever wonder if we're going too far, we're not. The only reason we got him is because we made his life hell for a few weeks. Then he realized that we actually had very valid issues. People do not care. The only way they will care is if we play hardball with them, and to please use him as an example.

When Tim Gunn was at Parsons the fur trade came in and gave a presentation. Tim had us in because he felt it was important that the animal side be represented too.

EM: Have you done other things besides interrupt runway shows?

DM: We've done some very colorful protests outside. We did a thing where we had a shot ring out several times with models with the slogan, "What if you were killed for your coat?" It was very gruesome.

We've had news conferences inside with personalities like Dennis Rodman, who unveiled his PETA campaign in the tents. He talked about how he had a problem with the animal cruelty involved. We were given a whole area in the tents. It got huge buzz.

We invested $20,000 to sponsor a show by Genevieve Gaelyn and Atom Cianfarani. They had a program where, instead of designing with leather, they gave kids a few bucks to gather up some inner tubes that were all over the city that were going to end up in landfills. They then used this industrial washer to clean the rubber and they used it in fashions. It was very innovative and very elegant. If you want a leather look use something like this instead of killing cows. They ended up getting rave reviews. I think it showed a lot of people that we'll invest in fashion to try to push people to do the right things as well.

EM: What would you like people to know about PETA?

DM: We are a charity. We're not for profit. We don't have an ad budget to speak of, so we have to get very creative to figure out how we can get our message across to the public and make our adversaries think twice about the things they're doing.

Dan in action

SPRING/SUMMER
2001
WAIST MANAGEMENT
PRESENTED SEPTEMBER 2000

EMPHASIS ON THE WAIST

BELTS WERE KEY for Spring/Summer 2001, as designers created silhouettes with the waist as the focal point.

Oscar de la Renta

Marc Jacobs

1980s

A WHIMSICAL TAKE on the 1980s; people who were born in that decade could now wear the styles, as could older generations who still had the original looks secretly packed away.

Victor Alfaro

Victor Alfaro

COMFORT AND EASE

THIS WAS A reaction to the luxury of Fall 2000. People wanted to relax and be comfortable. Designer logos began to disappear as well.

Luca Luca's shorts

Makeup at Oscar de la Renta

OTHER HIGHLIGHTS

Big hair at Oscar de la Renta

John Bartlett's wall of men

THE SCENE

★ Marc Jacobs debuted a new line, Marc by Marc Jacobs, at the Stuart Parr Gallery.

★ Kenneth Cole's show started off with a video from *The Daily Show with Jon Stewart*. In the video, politicians such as Hillary Clinton and Mario Cuomo encouraged people to vote.

★ The well-established label Escada made their New York Fashion Week debut this season. The show was held in conjunction with the G&P Foundation for Cancer Research, founded by Denise Rich and her son-in-law, Philip Aouad. Rich's daughter, Gabrielle Rich Aouad, had tragically died from acute myeloid leukemia (AML). While suffering from the disease, the foundation had been her dream as she wanted to find better treatment to help spare other cancer patients. G&P is named after Gabrielle and Philip.

★ The location for the Daryl K show was a working Chinatown bank. Designer Daryl Kerrigan and company had to wait until the bank closed at 3:00 in the afternoon before they could come in an hour later to prepare for the 8:00 show.

★ Callaghan showed in New York for the first time. Although the designer behind the London-based label was supposedly under wraps, it was widely known that it was Nicolas Ghesquière, who was backstage before the show.

★ Once again Betsey Johnson opted to not use runway models in her show. This season her collection was modeled by *Playboy* Bunnies.

★ Fashion Week regular Audrey Marnay was off the runways this season. She gave birth to her first child, a son, Amael, born on September 20, 2000.

★ While on jury duty, designer Kathlin Argiro cast some of her fellow jurors in her runway show.

Nicolas Ghesquière and Chloë Sevigny

Betsey Johnson and Playboy Bunnies

Oscar de la Renta and Gisele Bündchen

BETSEY JOHNSON

Designer Betsey Johnson broke into fashion by winning a guest editor spot at *Mademoiselle* in 1964. Her career took off and within a year she was designing professionally. She opened the boutique Betsey Bunki Nini in 1969. Her house model was Edie Sedgwick. Johnson has been designing ever since. She was given a special award by the CFDA for 1998–99. Johnson's cartwheel at the end of each runway show has become a Fashion Week tradition.

EILA MELL: How did you feel about the idea of a centralized show location at Bryant Park when it was first introduced?

BETSEY JOHNSON: I love the idea of all the shows being in the same venue. It's great to keep the editors in one place and not have all this run around. A lot of designers show in their showrooms, which breaks the "all together now" idea a bit. For me, I do like to mix it up—from showing in my backyard in East Hampton, to a club like Irving Plaza, our showroom cutting table, or a hotel like the Marquee or the Plaza.

EM: Do you see the runway as a type of theater?

BJ: It's totally theater! It's like a little dance recital or a little play. It has a theme, a concept, vignettes—a story. It's not to be the "hardcore seller" of clothes.

EM: One season you had *Playboy* models instead of runway models. Can you tell me about that decision and the reaction to the show?

BJ: Probably "best show ever." I've always wanted to work with the Playmates, and I was at a party in the city one night and it just hit me—the *Playboy* Playmates! It was a challenge because I had to work with the *Playboy* headquarters, but they were very pro, very supportive, very daring, and very courageous. It came out *beyond*! It was a big bang because that's when I announced my breast cancer too. That show was totally a three-ring circus. A dream come true was Hef [Hugh Hefner] sending me a personal note saying how much he loved the show.

EM: Are you your own muse?

BJ: I think so. I dream that I'm constantly eighteen, or twenty-five, or fifty-five—anything but my age!

EM: What would people be surprised to know about NY Fashion Week?

BJ: I still worry every season if I can do my cartwheel!

IMITATION OF CHRIST

For their debut show, Imitation of Christ designers Tara Subkoff and Matt Damhave staged a wake set in a real funeral parlor, the Peter Jarema Funeral Home. Models dressed as mourners took turns going up to the closed casket at the front of the room. Behind the scenes, creative director Chloë Sevigny worked to get the models ready before taking her front-row seat. The new label's show featured a T-shirt which read "Bring Me the Head of Tom Ford." A gracious Ford later congratulated Subkoff and Damhave, and even asked to buy the shirt.

FRESH FACE

RAICA OLIVEIRA

FROM: RIO DE JANEIRO, BRAZIL | HEIGHT: 5'10"
HAIR: BROWN | EYES: BROWN

Jill Stuart

FALL/WINTER
2001
PROPRIETY AND A RUNAWAY GOAT

PRESENTED FEBRUARY 2001

TRENDS:
MIX MASTERS

THERE WERE NO rules this season when it came to mixing prints, fabrics, and colors. Designers were unafraid to get it wrong, and presented combinations previously unseen on the runways.

Marc Jacobs

Diane Von Furstenberg

LADY-LIKE

A RETURN TO propriety was in the air—an aura exemplified by Jacqueline Kennedy Onassis. Fittingly, the Metropolitan Museum of Art was planning a new exhibition at the time called *Jacqueline Kennedy: The White House Years.*

MOD

Anna Sui

Anna Sui's stripes

Sheer at Luca Luca

OTHER HIGHLIGHTS

THE SCENE

★ Fashion-show newbie Melissa Etheridge attended the Calvin Klein show, where she was seated next to Hilary Swank.

★ Model Carmen Kass had a new experience at a runway show—she was a member of the audience.

★ Matchbox 20's Rob Thomas was at the tents watching his wife Marisol model in several shows.

★ Model Marcus Schenkenberg covered the shows for NBC's *Extra*.

★ Actor Alan Cumming was originally scheduled to appear in Cynthia Rowley's show. He had to drop out, but showed up in the audience to support Rowley nevertheless.

★ Kenneth Cole asked his guests to bring clothing to his show to donate to the homeless. He also screened an animated video in which Kathy Griffin asked celebrities for donations.

★ Miguel Adrover's collection for Pegasus Apparel was inspired by a recent trip in which he spent six weeks in Egypt. In his show Adrover had a woman lead a goat onto the runway. The goat had a mind of its own and refused to walk. Finally, Stephen Ruzow, the chairman of Pegasus Apparel, tried to control the situation and jumped onto the runway in an effort to calm the goat. The goat obviously had no aspirations to be a model and opted to hide under the runway instead of walking the walk.

★ During the preceding season, Stephen Slowik had been chosen to take over design at Bill Blass. His tenure lasted only a single season. A month before the Fall 2001 show Bill Blass staff designer Lars Nilsson was hired as Slowik's replacement.

★ Both Imitation of Christ co-designer Tara Subkoff and creative director Chloë Sevigny were actresses. Fittingly, the label's presentation was staged as a movie premiere held at the Clearview Theater on 66th Street. Guests were asked to donate money to Sweatshop Watch and Free the Children. Live footage of models arriving at the premiere in the label's designs was shown. The models then made their way into the theater, where a short film with performances by Reese Witherspoon and Selma Blair was shown. Simultaneously, in a corner of the screen a documentary was also shown.

Imitation of Christ

Phillip Bloch and Sofia Vergara

EDMUNDO CASTILLO

Edmundo Castillo came to New York from his native Puerto Rico to pursue his career as a shoe designer. He worked for Donna Karan and Ralph Lauren before launching his eponymous line. In addition, Castillo was creative director of Sergio Rossi. In 2001 he was awarded the prestigious Swarovski's Perry Ellis Award for Accessory Design from the CFDA.

EILA MELL: You worked for Donna Karan very early in your career. How did you get such a great job so soon?

EDMUNDO CASTILLO: I had interviews with all of New York, basically; shoe designers and fashion designers; I did internships. I started at Oscar de la Renta decorating shoes from past seasons. There were a lot of shoe designers I didn't have enough experience to work for. Then I ran into Donna Karan at my roommate's Parsons graduation fashion show, at which Donna was a critic. I was trying to get to Donna but I didn't know how. I found myself bumping into her as I was going down the stairs and she was coming out. I didn't hesitate to tell her that I loved what she was doing and I would love to show her my shoes. She told me to call Josh Patner. At the time he was dealing with the licensees at Donna Karan. The shoe section was a licensee. I never got to Josh. So I kept trying to get to her, but I couldn't. Finally, someone helped me get an interview with someone that happened to be the wrong person. By mistake I ended up speaking with a shoe designer. It was a Friday, and she took me to see Donna and showed her my book. They told me they had to think about it and would give me a call in two weeks. I had heard that story so many times. But as I was walking out I found out they hired me! I was twenty-one.

EM: What was it like working with Donna Karan?

EC: I immediately connected with her. Everything that I am now I owe to Donna in a big way. She was that dream designer to work for. We were a very close team. She was extremely open minded. She was eager for you to discover and experiment. As a design director recently in Italy I tried to create the same kind of team.

Candy Pratts Price was another very strong influence. She picked up where Donna left off.

EM: What's the difference between designing men and women's shoes?

EC: You design men's shoes more practically. Men are very particular about their shoes. A woman's shoe is about dreams and fantasy and unpracticality. It's an emotion. I love the psychology of shoes. It's more about what it does to people, how it transforms internally. I've always called shoes makeup for the feet.

EM: What did winning the CFDA award mean to you?

EC: It was recognition of all my hard work and passion.

EM: What inspired you to relaunch your shoe line, Edmundo Castillo?

EC: I started running into women in New York with some of my shoes from 2003, 2004. I started seeing pictures in *The Sartorialist* of a beautiful Giovanna Battaglia walking in Paris on two different occasions in two different pairs of my shoes. I sat next to a woman at a restaurant. I looked down and she was wearing one of my flat sandals. It really was fabulously satisfying because it was the first time I saw the results of what I was trying to build when I started my collection. The

"I have the utmost respect for Edmundo Castillo's talent and his vision.
His precision and knowledge of shoe design and manufacturing is what draws me to his work."
—Narciso Rodriguez

shoes looked fresh. They didn't look dated.

EM: What are some of the more unusual things you've tried as a shoe designer?

EC: I did a shoe to experiment with new technology. It turns on. It's made of light. It was an attempt to do something new without being extravagant. To make something new and fun, something people would want to buy to look at—a shoe you turn on, with a bottom you recharge with a USB cable. You can recharge it to the computer, the car lighter, the wall.

EM: Are there any rules when it comes to shoes?

EC: For women it's all about wearing what you feel most feminine in. That could be a ballerina slipper, a motorcycle boot, a stiletto, or a hooker pump. Whatever makes you feel good regardless of what people think.

EM: How important is comfort when designinng a shoe?

EC: Comfort is key; comfort is also relative. A heel could be five inches. If you're used to wearing a five-inch heel you'd be comfortable. It's very important that a high heel fits in a certain way. It's important that the foot sits in three points in a high heel, not just in the front. It's very important that the arch is curved in a certain way. I like a shoe that is pretty on the table and gorgeous on the foot. The way a shoe fits is what makes the shoe take over and speak the way it should. The posture of the woman becomes more confident. A heel should never feel as high as it really is. The comfort of the shoe is what does that.

EM: Any favorite memories of New York Fashion Week?

EC: When Bryant Park first started the runways were elevated. It was exciting that people could see the shoes. I love the smell of fashion in the air during Fashion Week. The city's buzzing. Nothing's more exciting than New York fashion. It's a community, not a competition.

FRESH
FACES

ERIN WASSON

FROM: IRVINE, TEXAS | HEIGHT: 5'10½"
HAIR: BLONDE | EYES: HAZEL

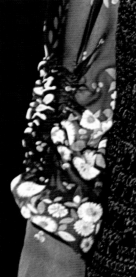

NATALIA VODIANOVA

FROM: NIZHNY, NOVGOROD, RUSSIA | HEIGHT: 5'9½"
HAIR: BROWN | EYES: BLUE

Paris and Nicky Hilton

PETA protest

Johnnie Cochran (left)

SNAPPED!

Kimora Lee

Kal Ruttenstein and Janice Combs

SEPTEMBER 11, 2001

ON TUESDAY, SEPTEMBER 11, 2001, AT 8:46 AM, AMERICAN AIRLINES FLIGHT 11 CRASHED into the World Trade Center's North Tower, killing everyone on board. At that moment the world did not know that the plane had been hijacked by al-Qaeda terrorists. Seventeen minutes later, the situation became much more ominous, as United Airlines Flight 175 crashed into the South Tower. At that moment the country knew something was very wrong.

Life was proceeding as normal at the Bryant Park tents early that morning. The Liz Lange maternity show was about to begin. Just before the show, people learned that a plane had crashed into the World Trade Center. No one knew the circumstances, and the show went on as planned. It was not until afterwards that people learned about the second crash. Fern Mallis asked for everyone's attention and announced that the World Trade Center had collapsed and the Pentagon had been hit. She urged the crowd to find their loved ones and be safe. Only the most necessary staff remained at the tents to secure the millions of dollars worth of equipment. The staff at the park was having trouble reaching IMG, who had just bought 7th on Sixth, making them the new owners of New York Fashion Week. They shipped thousands of boxes of Evian (a Fashion Week sponsor) to Ground Zero, and also went down there to help create tents.

"That afternoon we were running through the tents, out of the tents, down 40th Street," said Mallis. "There were bomb scares left and right. I remember running with security, and people were losing their shoes and we're wondering where we're running to. It was horrible. Somebody came then, one of the guys, and put a big American flag in front of the tent. Then we turned the tent into somewhat of a retrieval center for a little while with products and things for people gathering. Nobody knew what was needed. Everybody thought there were going to be millions of people who needed stuff, and nobody needed stuff because there was nobody there. It was horrible. The season shut down."

Two other planes were also hijacked that tragic day. At 9:37 AM, American Airlines Flight 77 hit the Pentagon. United Airlines Flight 93 crashed near Shanksville, Pennsylvania. The heroic passengers on board saved countless lives by attempting to overtake the hijackers. As a result, the plane crashed into a field rather than its unknown intended target.

This was not a day for fashion shows.

America was changed.

DKNY

FALL/WINTER
2002
A RETURN TO THE TENTS
PRESENTED FEBRUARY 2002

Fall/Winter 2002 was the first season after September 11, 2001.
There was no Spring/Summer 2002 season. Fall 2002 was a transitional season
of the unknown. It was a confusing time for designers. No one wanted to be showy.
Designers realized that people didn't necessarily want to see fashion, but they
still had businesses to run. Nobody felt comfortable. Nobody wanted excess of
any kind. Nobody knew if anyone was even going to shop. Many designers
skipped the Bryant Park tents and had small presentations in their showrooms
instead. Fear was in the air. Everybody scaled back. The trends of
Fall/Winter 2002 were a clear reflection of the somber mood at the time.

TRENDS:
LONG SKIRTS

Oscar de la Renta

Balenciaga

LAYERING

SLOUCH

Jill Stuart

Rick Owens

Simon Doonan and his dog Liberace at Perry Ellis

Donna Karan Collection's wine-stained lips, model: Erin Wasson

Jill Stuart's scarf

Multi-colored eyes at Anna Sui

OTHER HIGHLIGHTS

Michael Kors sunglasses, model: Gabriel Aubry

Patrick McMullan

Balenciaga's clean faces

THE SCENE

★ With a red, white, and blue banner designed by Stephen Sprouse as a backdrop, Mayor Michael Bloomberg cut the ribbon to officially kick off Fashion Week. Bloomberg stated that the best way to honor those who were lost on September 11, 2001 was to go forward.

★ This was the first full season to be run by IMG instead of the CFDA. CFDA president Stan Herman on why they sold to IMG: "Each year the shows got bigger and bigger and it had gotten too difficult for us to manage. Fern became the voice of it. As the president of the council I personally felt Fashion Week was sucking the life out of the CFDA. We started to think somebody might be interested in it. IMG became the big interest. It was [IMG president] Chuck Bennett who I dealt with and sold it to. If we didn't I would have closed it because we were beginning to bleed. We had to hire more people and have more offices. When you looked at the bottom line it wasn't working for the CFDA, as a non-profit organization."

★ Bob Mackie celebrated musical theater with his Fall 2002 collection. He displayed designs based on *My Fair Lady*, *Annie Get Your Gun*, *Mame*, and *Hello Dolly!*

★ Top hairstylist Eugene Souleiman made his New York Fashion Week debut. Souleiman's shows included Ralph Lauren, DKNY, Narciso Rodriguez, BCBG MaxAzria, and Rick Owens.

★ Designer Nicolas Ghesquiere brought the Spanish label Balenciaga to New York. Among the familiar faces in his audience were Sarah Jessica Parker and Anna Wintour.

★ Sydney Biddle Barrows, who became known as the Mayflower Madam in 1984, was the dresser at the Luca Luca and Custo Barcelona shows.

★ The Pierrot show featured the fairy-tale characters Little Red Riding Hood, Rapunzel, Snow White, and Snow White's stepmother, the evil queen (played by Carmen Dell'Orrefice).

★ Baseball stars Derek Jeter and Mo Vaughn came out to see the Marc Jacobs show.

★ Designers looking to book Gisele Bündchen for their shows were told that she was unavailable. They were not too happy when Bündchen made a single exception to walk the runway for Luella Bartley.

★ Betsey Johnson's show was held in her workroom. Her runway was her cutting table and she had twenty-two of her staff members as models. The designer on why she decided to go that route: "It was the show right after 9/11, and everyone was terrified about money. I felt people needed an up-close and personal, but truly fun experience. Buyers and press sat behind the sewing machines in the cutting room, and all our employees modeled on the cutting table. I danced and commentated all the way through. I wanted to do a feel-good, inexpensive show or no show at all. I mean it was that kind of time zone when a lot of people didn't show."

★ Marc Bouwer's show was sponsored by PETA. The designer showed fake fur in his collection. After the show, a song called "Don't Kill the Animals" was played.

★ Shu Uemura signed up to be the sole beauty sponsor for Fall 2002.

★ Special Appearances: Patrick McMullan, Simon Doonan, and Ethan Zohn at Perry Ellis.

TY YORIO

A former New York City Detective, Ty Yorio has headed the team responsible for the security of New York Fashion Week since it began in 1993.

EILA MELL: How do you and your team keep New York Fashion Week safe?

TY YORIO: As the saying goes, "How do you get to Carnegie Hall? Practice, practice." That's what keeps Fashion Week secure. From the very onset, in November 1993, it was evident that there would be throngs of people passing through the doors of the tents. It immediately became one of the hottest tickets in town. Collaborating with the architects that design the venues and the personnel that build the tents requires continual "tweaking" to create the optimum fashion village for all.

Security officers are positioned at every key location to greet authorized designer personnel and guide them to their appropriate venues. The front door and check-in desks are one of the most important aspects of the assignment. Designers are allocated a certain number of credentials for backstage entry as we must be compliant with all New York City building codes with regard to capacity. Officers also keep out the unauthorized and uninvited. During an eight-day Fashion Week, lobby security personnel can process more than 100,000 guests and support staff past their assigned posts. Security reserves the right to inspect all bags, attaché cases, luggage, etc., that is within our "footprint."

Security needs to be constantly vigilant but also maintain a presence that blends into the fabric of the event. Security is there to facilitate the events of the day and never to overshadow those events in any way.

EM: What was it like to be working security the morning of September 11?

TY: It was the fifth day of Fashion Week. I remember when the first plane roared down Fifth Avenue, flying dangerously low directly over our heads, causing me and other security officers to comment, "What was that?" The first show of the day was Liz Lange Maternity, which filled our lobby with hundreds of expectant moms. I recall thinking it ironic seeing all those moms to be, and then stepping outside the tents and looking south along Sixth Avenue, witnessing the destruction of thousands of innocent souls.

At approximately 8:55 AM, while speaking with officers of the Midtown South Precinct, their beepers started to go off, and I witnessed their expressions as they called the precinct and were informed that an airliner had struck the north tower of the World Trade Center. Before we could even process that news we learned that another airliner had struck the south tower. It became evident that we were under attack, and fear of the unknown set in. Bryant Park placed us two blocks south of Times Square, one block west of Grand Central Station, and five blocks west of the United Nations Building. Any of these locales could be targeted. The designer of the first show personally came to me and asked if I could guarantee the safety of her guests, to which I replied, "I cannot guarantee their safety." The lobby was filled with hundreds of pregnant attendees patiently waiting to enter when the call was made to suspend all shows for the day.

Through my contacts with The NYC Police Department I was able to stay current with the unfolding events minute by minute, which was a tremendous help. We evacuated all areas of our footprint in Bryant Park. I then began assessing requests of security personnel within the tents who wanted to leave to be with their families. As certain non-essential personnel departed we became a rendezvous/staging area for the police and other citizens. Eventually we made contact with the Office of Emergency Management of the City of New York and it was determined that all subsequent shows that week would be cancelled. Later that morning I recall hearing and seeing U.S. Air Force Fighter Jets flying over Manhattan and feeling a measure of safety, but also realizing that the world had changed forever.

ON THE SCENE

FACES

SARA ZIFF

FROM: NEW YORK, NY | HEIGHT: 5'11"
HAIR: BLONDE | EYES: BLUE/GREY

EVA JAY KUBATOVA

FROM: CZECH REPUBLIC | HEIGHT: 5'11"
HAIR: BLONDE | EYES: BLUE/GREEN

ANA BELA SANTOS

FROM: SÃO PAULO, BRAZIL | HEIGHT: 5'10"
HAIR: BROWN | EYES: BROWN

Anna Wintour

Donna Karan and Marcelle Bittarrs

Derek Jeter

SNAPPED!

Donna Karan, model: Isabeli Fontana

SPRING/SUMMER
2003
A PRETTY SEASON
PRESENTED SEPTEMBER 2002

TRENDS: SPORTY

A SEXY, SPORTY feel was in the air for Spring/Summer 2003.

Anna Sui, model: Audrey Marnay

Michael Kors, model: Carmen Kass

1950s

THIS SEASON AUDIENCES saw softer, pretty silhouettes as people began to embrace the idea of dressing up again following the tragedies of 9/11.

Marc Jacobs

Ralph Lauren

METALLICS

SPRING/SUMMER 2003 **183**

Diane von Furstenberg's bangles

Pierrot's family

Jeremy Scott's leaves

OTHER
HIGHLIGHTS

Anna Sui's headband

Soft makeup at Ralph Lauren

THE SCENE

★ The Maurice Villency store on 57th Street was the setting for the Imitation of Christ retrospective show. On one floor topless models in cashmere underwear vacuumed the floor, while downstairs tapes of the three-year-old label's old shows were seen on the walls.

★ Heatherette designers Richie Rich and Traver Rains introduced a new girl on the runway—Hello Kitty. Her iconic image appeared on items ranging from dresses to chaps.

★ Betsey Johnson showed her collection before the official start of Fashion Week. On August 10, Johnson's show was presented at her East Hampton home. Guests spent the day celebrating not only the collection, but Johnson's twenty-fourth year in the fashion industry and her sixtieth birthday.

★ To celebrate his thirty-fifth anniversary in fashion, Ralph Lauren erected a large tent in the gardens of the Cooper-Hewitt Museum. Crystal chandeliers, plush cushions, candles, champagne, and the music of Erik Satie set a romantic tone that his Spring 2003 collection echoed.

★ Actress Alicia Silverstone attended her first ever fashion show at Anne Klein this season.

★ Nicole Miller and Badgley Mischka both chose to show in showrooms at 525 Seventh Avenue. An elevator carrying guests from one to the other got stuck in between floors when a cable snapped. *InStyle* editor Toby Tucker was among those trapped inside. She managed to free herself by climbing her way out.

★ The hit British series *Absolutely Fabulous* shot an episode at designer Jared Gold's show. Actresses Jennifer Saunders and Joanna Lumley's characters, Patsy and Edina, travel to New York and attend Fashion Week in the episode titled "Gay."

★ Special Appearance: Paris Hilton walking for Pierrot.

Paris Hilton   *Imitation of Christ*   *Ralph Lauren*   *Heatherette*

NEW
ON THE
SCENE

M.R.S.

Makeup artist Molly R. Stern had her first runway show for her line, m.r.s. (her initials) at Barney's Co-Op store in Soho. The theme for the show was the 1953 Marilyn Monroe-Betty Grable-Lauren Bacall film *How to Marry a Millionaire*. Each outfit had a name, like "The Mediterranean Stroller" and "The Saturday Night Swisher."

FRESH
FACES

BRIGITTE SWIDRAK

FROM: JEFFERSON, NEW JERSEY
HEIGHT: 5'10" | HAIR: BROWN | EYES: BLUE/GREEN

IRIS STRUBEGGER

FROM: SALZBURG, AUSTRIA | HEIGHT: 5'11"
HAIR: BROWN | EYES: BLUE

Austrian model Iris Strubegger has been the face of Balenciaga, Valentino, Karl Lagerfeld, MaxMara, and Givenchy. She has walked the runways for just about every top designer, and has been on the cover of numerous magazines, including *V* and *French Vogue*.

"Calvin Klein was my first big, international show, and to be honest I had no idea what was happening to me. When I think back I still can't believe it happened. It was simply amazing."
—Iris Strubegger

EILA MELL: How did you start modeling?

IRIS STRUBEGGER: I was scouted on the streets of New York while I was staying there for a student exchange.

EM: What's a typical Fashion Week like for you?

IS: It's busy and exhausting, but I love it. Every new appointment, fitting, and show gives me so much energy and so much to look forward to. To be part of the process makes me happy and proud. Not many girls are able to experience what I do.

EM: How did cutting your hair impact your career?

IS: My haircut was the best thing that could have happened to my career. It was cut for the cover of the March 2009 issue of French *Vogue*. The short hair gave my look something unique and outstanding.

EM: How big an issue is a model's weight?

IS: A designer works with different materials, cuts, and colors. Models work with their bodies so of course it's important for us to look a certain way. The problem for most girls is finding a way to stay healthy, both physically and mentally, and thin at the same time. This is a big issue in my eyes.

EM: What's it like to open or close a show?

IS: It is a big honor for a model to open or close a show. It happens when a model's look represents the inspiration and idea of a designer's collection. It's an amazing feeling to be sort of an inspiration or muse for a designer and even more amazing to be chosen to be their first or last face in a show.

EM: What do you love most about your job?

IS: Meeting and working with so many interesting, inspiring, and creative people.

EM: How is Fashion Week in New York different from in other cities?

IS: I think New York is a great city to start the Fashion Weeks. I can always feel the great energy that is pulsing in this city all year long; during Fashion Week, I feel it even stronger. The designers are young and energetic or classic and timeless, just like New York itself!

EM: Any favorite moments from Bryant Park?

IS: To be able to be part of Naomi Campbell's show, Relief for Haiti.

EM: What would people be surprised to know about New York Fashion Week?

IS: That by metro it's so much faster and easier to make your appointments on time than it is by taxi!

NIAN FISH

Nian Fish is the creative director and senior vice president of KCD Worldwide, a leading fashion PR and production agency. She has produced runway shows for many leading designers, such as Calvin Klein, Marc Jacobs, Ralph Lauren, Zac Posen, and Gucci.

EILA MELL: What's Fashion Week like for you?

NIAN FISH: People say Fashion Week, but it's actually fashion month. I have often worked in three cities, sometimes four—New York, Milan, Paris, and London. The fourth city, London, is a killer. From February to March I work every night until midnight, plus every single weekend without a day off. It feels like you're doing in a month what anybody else would do in a year.

EM: What about the weeks leading up to that month?

NF: I'm a creative director and a producer. It's an unusual combination. The first thing we do is pick a timeslot and a location. The timeslot's really important. After that you start building the team, which is centered on the stylist. In the early 1990s the stylist became critical. That wasn't so before then. Designers would style their own collections for the most part. It was very rare for a stylist to come in and tell the designer what blouse goes with what skirt. There's also hair and makeup, music, casting, set design. Sometimes I will be the set designer.

EM: Why has the stylist become so crucial?

NF: My opinion is they use stylists now because they have so much pressure to become a global brand image that a lot of times they cannot have the creative time to put those things together. Not just physically, but even the wherewithal to know what's going on in fashion, doing their homework, and knowing where to bring the brand forward. It's really become the stylist's job to push the brand forward and create the trend for them—to either be part of a trend or create a new one. It's really important that the stylist can carry the designer's vision through, in sometimes a higher way than they might have thought before.

EM: Marc Jacobs is usually a big trendsetter.

NF: Marc Jacobs is an amazing stylist. Part of what makes him so successful is that he embraces every aspect of what he needs to do to make a great show, from the venue, to set design, styling, and casting. He just has that gift. But he does have a wonderful stylist with him, too. They've been working together for years and years.

Designing a collection is one part, but the styling of it, deciding which girl goes in which outfit, what music she is walking out to, everything. I always say we're creating theater.

EM: So theatricality is important?

NF: Theatricality is prime, even if you just have a white background. That white background is there because you wouldn't want a painted Renaissance backdrop behind a Calvin Klein show. The fact that he uses a white minimalistic background, that's theater. It tells you about the brand immediately. If it's white cold light or yellow light, all of these things have a subliminal message that communicates to the audience. Fashion shows are basically entertainment. It's not a secret that many things on the runway are not sold. Some say it's all smoke and mirrors. Most of the people who do the lighting design, staging, and sound come from and still do theater, but they find fashion more lucrative.

EM: How has fashion changed in the recent past?

NF: The creativity and passion in our business never ceases to amaze me. Fashion isn't what it used to be, it's true. This is a time of conglomerates and licensees and branding the designer to be able to sell that perfume, those sunglasses. When I started it really was about the clothes. It was about the designer, but now it's about the image.

EM: What is the business like for a new designer?

NF: The instant reviews on the web permeate to the entire world instantly. If that young designer fails everyone knows about it. I almost think that new designers shouldn't get reviewed. It's a testimony to the ones who have survived not great press in the beginning. Too much is expected of them to be an overnight hit. People forget it took Calvin Klein years to develop his identity.

EM: Any memories that stand out from New York Fashion Week?

NF: I witnessed Calvin Klein himself changing the hem length on every single girl. It got deemed the new length, which is right below the knee. He had called every girl up to get that redone. We were there; we didn't sleep. We finished the last fitting at 7 AM. The girls had to go right into hair and makeup. It was right though. He did the right thing.

SNAPPED!

Angie Harmon

Pierre Carrilero

Anna Sui and Naomi Campbell

Marc Jacobs

FALL/WINTER

2003

A MOD SEASON

PRESENTED FEBRUARY 2003

TRENDS:
1960s

FASHION WORKED ITS way through the decades from previous season's '50s fling to Fall 2003's visit to the 1960s. This time around audiences saw the sweeter side of the era. This was more Belle du Jour, less Hair.

Carolina Herrera

Marc Jacobs

SATIN

A MODERN TAKE on the 1930s was shown—a very Jean Harlow moment on the runway.

SHORT SKIRTS

VERY SHORT SKIRTS were shown, often with tights or leggings.

Marc Jacobs

Matthew Williamson, model: Fernanda Taveras

Pink lips at Cynthia Steffe

Fusha's bun

OTHER HIGHLIGHTS

Red lipstick at Carolina Herrera

Diane von Furstenberg's makeup

Kenneth Cole's boots

THE SCENE

★ Iconic designer Calvin Klein showed his final collection for Fall 2003. Klein sold his company to the Phillips-Van Heusen Corporation but said he would have a role in the company as a consulting creative director.

★ There was plenty to do in between shows. The Evian café was serving pizza if anyone was hungry. Those looking for a mini makeover could go over to the booth with Shu Uemura's makeup artists or even get a pedicure at a Dr. Scholl's booth.

★ Sean Combs hired Lori Goldstein to style his eight women's looks for his Sean John show. Reportedly, the two disagreed on the styling of an outfit, and Goldstein was let go.

★ The Gap was giving out blue canvas tote bags to Fashion Week attendees outside the tents.

★ *Elle* magazine put up taxi kiosks near Bryant Park and other show venues to make travel easier for guests.

★ Bill Blass designer Lars Nilsson showed his collection on a Wednesday. On Thursday the surprise announcement came that he was let go from the company. There was buzz that Bill Blass chief executive Michael Groveman had a replacement, Michael Vollbracht, already lined up.

★ Imitation of Christ brought its audience to the circus. Designer Tara Subkoff's invitation to the show at Pier 63 came in an envelope with confetti and a peanut. In addition to the fashions offered, Subkoff's guests were also entertained by circus performers.

★ Jeremy Scott's show was quite an event. It was held at the Tribeca Grand Hotel, and was a takeoff on Hollywood awards shows. Models and celebrities (China Chow, Lisa Marie) walked a red carpet and were interviewed by Scott. Afterward, Scott presented a short film called *Starring*. Chow and Marie appeared in the film, along with Tori Spelling, Amber Valletta, and Monet Mazur.

Calvin Klein

Nicole Miller

LAUREN EZERSKY

For almost ten years Lauren Ezersky hosted the popular series *Behind the Velvet Ropes*, where she took viewers behind the scenes of the fashion world. Ezersky has been an on-air correspondent for the show *Fashion File* and a columnist for *Paper* magazine.

EILA MELL: What was it like before the shows were centralized at Bryant Park?

LAUREN EZERSKY: I remember starting out going to all the hotels that used to have the shows, like the Pierre and the Plaza, and it was so elegant and fabulous. And now it's like going to the supermarket. We have a barcode. It's ridiculous.

EM: Can you tell me about being in Betsey Johnson's show?

LE: I love Betsey. She's the best. Well, it was really fun. Betsey just lets you do your thing. Because at one point models would just stomp down the runway; they all looked totally miserable. You know, Betsey puts you in some really fun clothes and makes you feel great. Great makeup and hair, and it's just fun. It's like you're at a party, not work. So I enjoyed doing anything for her, as a favor or whatever, because she's a friend too. She's a fun lady and ageless.

EM: She is amazing. How did that come about, that you were asked to be in the show?

LE: Betsey is into real people. She knew me and I guess I have my own style and she likes people who are individuals because she's such an individual. She asked me if I would do it. Every now and then she'll do the non-model or just add some regular people in. I adore her. She's really nice to deal with—just one of the sweetest people. A lot of these younger designers have attitude already and they're in the business for only a couple of years or a year. Let them see if they can be in business forty years. That's a feat that's hard to accomplish.

EM: Were you there on September 11?

LE: I was. I was actually right in the middle of an interview with Douglas Hannant.

EM: Was there a somber mood returning the next season?

LE: Oh my God, yes. But you know—we've never forgotten, we won't forget, but you just have to move on.

EM: Were you there when *Unzipped* was being shot?

LE: I guess I've been around for everything. But you just don't really pay attention. It's like this whirlwind hurricane that just keeps sucking everything in. You do your thing, everybody does their thing and that's the way it is. And that's what makes it such an exciting business, because you're not bored. There's always something different. Every day is different; every season is different.

EM: Can you tell me about your show, *Behind the Velvet Rope*?

LE: I was a guest on a show which was in existence then called *Behind the Velvet Rope*. It was three different people that did it. It was on fashion, movies, and music. We did it for five years for no money. Everybody just kind of came together for the love of it. And then no one was making money, everybody wanted to leave, and I was the only one who wanted to keep doing it. I went out and got a sponsor. I just did it. We shot a couple of episodes, put it on the air. I had eight years with that.

I'd love to bring it back because people still seem to want it, but all they're airing is reality shows. No one seems to want to know about designers anymore. It's about who's wearing the designer. I love designers; I think they're like artists.

EM: Why do you think fashion has become so mainstream?

LE: It's shows like *Project Runway*. It's stores like Gap having designers design T-shirts and stuff for them, as well as having people like Sarah Jessica Parker as, you know, the spokesgirl or the muse. Karl Lagerfeld is designing for H&M. Everybody wants to wear a label, and if you can't afford the genuine Karl Lagerfeld or Chanel then you can go to H&M with fifty bucks and buy something.

I think the media has really helped because there are so many cameras out there now and everybody wants to look good. And you don't have to spend a lot of money at all to look good anymore.

EM: There was a season when the shows moved to Chelsea Piers.

LE: I didn't like that. It was really out of the way. It's just not convenient. And you're working, you're doing stuff. You might have to go back to the office, and people don't have budgets anymore to take a cab or a car service. I mean, I never did. You have to take public transportation and it takes time. So you can't have a back-to-back show at 3:00 PM and then go to something uptown at 4:00. You're not going to make it. I think it's still like that. Now you have Lincoln Center and then you have studios like Milk. So, you know, it's still far apart from each other. I think some designers will lose because you can't do everything.

EM: It's too bad everybody doesn't just show in one space for convenience.

LE: Well, you would think, but every one of these designers want to be creative and I understand that too, and they can't all afford the tents because it's pricey. I think in Europe it's different; they get subsidized, but here they don't. It's expensive even to do a little show. You have to pay the models, even if you give them clothes or something. Everything costs money, and it's just not that easy anymore.

EM: What's the most fun part about covering Fashion Week?

LE: The most fun part is discovering a new designer or seeing a beautiful collection. And when I'm sitting there I'm just speechless because I know I can't do that. I'm thinking "How did they think of this? How did they make this?" The hair, the makeup, is so beautiful. And then when I interview someone and hear their point of view, and see it on the air, and people say they liked it—that makes my day.

NEW
ON THE
SCENE

Doo.Ri Chung

Marie Claudinette Pierre-Jean (left)

DOO.RI

Doo.Ri Chung made her runway debut for Fall/Winter 2003. Chung, a 1995 graduate of Parsons School of Design, previously worked as head designer for Geoffrey Beene. In 2001 she started her line, Doo.Ri in the basement of her parents' dry-cleaning business.

FUSHA

Marie Claudinette Pierre-Jean called her Fusha line "French-Caribbean couture." The wife of music artist Wyclef Jean, her supporters included Patti LaBelle and Ben Vereen.

Derek Lam

Lazaro Hernandez and Jack McCollough

DEREK LAM

Former Michael Kors designer Derek Lam premiered his eponymous line this season. The San Francisco native graduated Parsons in 1990.

PROENZA SCHOULER

Designers Jack McCollough and Lazaro Hernandez's first Proenza Schouler show was presented at the National Arts Club. The pair met while studying at Parsons, and collaborated on their senior thesis collection, which was bought, in its entirety, by Barneys.

FRESH FACES

TIIU KUIK

FROM: TALLINN, ESTONIA | HEIGHT: 6'
HAIR: BLONDE | EYES: BROWN/GREEN

VANESSA PERRON

FROM: LAC SAINT-JEAN, QUEBEC
HEIGHT: 5' 10'' | HAIR: BROWN | EYES: BLUE

BEN GRIMES-VIORT

FROM: LONDON, ENGLAND | HEIGHT: 5' 8½"
HAIR: BROWN | EYES: BLUE

Carolina Herrera

SPRING/SUMMER
2004
VACATION MODE
PRESENTED SEPTEMBER 2003

TRENDS:
SURF STYLE

SPRING 2004 WAS fun-filled with bright colors. Surf style offered loose hair, bikinis, cover-ups, and the inviting idea of being on vacation 24/7.

Anna Sui

Oscar de la Renta

NAUTICAL

THE MORE DRESSED up, yachting side of surf style.

SHORTS

Tommy Hilfiger

Kenneth Cole

Pink lips at Oscar de la Renta

Zac Posen's necklace

OTHER HIGHLIGHTS

Highlight in the corner of the eye at Carolina Herrera

Kenneth Cole's menswear

MÝA

In addition to being a Grammy-winning singer, Mýa is also a songwriter and a record producer. Her acting credits include roles in the films *Shall We Dance* and *Chicago*. Mýa has also walked the runway at New York Fashion Week on occasion.

EILA MELL: I know that you love fashion. You even chose to go to Fashion Week over the Grammys one year.

MÝA: Well, I just was a part of the Grammys, I believe it may have been 2002 or 2003, and I was focusing on music again, but behind the scenes. So I chose Fashion Week because I wasn't going to perform at the Grammys. I didn't think I necessarily had to be there. I'd like to be useful if I was going to be at an awards show.

EM: Do you have a favorite designer whose show you don't like to miss?

M: I loved Heatherette. It's not just the clothes. It's a production, with performances, and a theme, always. I think my favorite Heatherette show was when they had Hello Kitty as their theme and it was very Raggedy Ann. A lot of plaids, like Dorothy from *Wizard of Oz* meets *Hello Kitty*, meets pregnant-girl smoking cigarettes on the runway—very edgy. They loved to make statements. Heatherette was a production, and I'm into theater. I love fashion shows that focus not only on the clothes and the collection, but a theme as well. It's entertaining.

EM: What's the celebrity Fashion Week experience?

M: Well, there are gifting suites at every Fashion Week, and you get spoiled and pampered, all kinds of certificates. You also get to meet the designers backstage and speak with them about their collection; go to their showrooms afterward, maybe when all the clothes have been returned from the models hopefully you can get into a sample size—which is why I always fast before Fashion Week! There are a lot of parties, which can be dangerous if you're trying to attend a lot of shows because they interfere with your sleep schedule. It's best to get a lot of rest. But I don't think that's realistic during Fashion Week because there is way too much to do.

EM: What are the gifting suites like? Like Christmas morning?

M: Well, sometimes these were actually set up in the tents at Bryant Park—certain alcoholic beverages, certain bottles given with your name and crystals. There are also spa certificates and mobile spa units set up; you can get manicures, pedicures. There are booths set up from hairstylists, and companies that provide you with products after you've obtained their services. It's a week of pampering, entertainment, and excitement.

EM: So what's bad about that, huh?

M: It's really not bad at all. You have to prioritize. You may skip a few shows to get pampered. When you're in entertainment there's always something going on for you—whether it's a PSA, speaking engagement, an appearance, performance, a tour—and you'd like to be well informed of what's coming out soon to give you ideas about your wardrobe—maybe make a knock off of a famous dress! Or you can speak with the designers themselves about working with you on a project exclusively. It's a sneak peek of what's to come.

EM: So, when you're attending are you there to get inspired?

M: I am. I'm getting ideas, taking snapshots with my cell phone camera. A lot of things are so nonrealistic that you may never want to wear them on the street unless you're seeking attention during Halloween, but if you are in entertainment there is always a place where you can be outrageous. So I'm also shopping, but it's largely about getting inspired and getting ideas.

EM: When a designer invites you to their show do they also dress you for that show?

M: Some designers, Tommy Hilfiger in the past has allowed a couple of artists, including myself, to come to his showroom and pick out a few things from his collection that he'll be debuting, and we'll wear it at his fashion show. A lot of designers don't want you to show up in something else, you know, out of respect so it is best to get with them or their team, and appear in their design or their collection.

EM: So if you're going to more than one show in a day do you need to bring a change of clothes?

M: I change in the car during Fashion Week—my hair, nails, makeup, all right there. I had to get used to that, because you miss shows. A lot of them go overtime. You have to be prepared. I'll go to my hotel before the after party, but I want to absorb as much information as possible, so I go to my SUV between shows. It's quicker than going back to the hotel.

EM: Talk about some designers whose shows you go to. Let's start with Rag and Bone.

M: You can actually wear their clothes on an everyday basis. It has a little bit of edge, denim—you know, funky, fresh, youthful. I love it.

E: How about Baby Phat?

M: Baby Phat is fabulous. I love the colors that Kimora brings every year no matter if it's a winter collection, fall, or spring. Usually in the summer/spring there's a lot more yellows and brighter colors, but she's fun year round. The accessories are always on point to compliment the outfits. She has the whole nine yards—from the hair, to makeup, shoes, everything is coordinated and it not only features the attire but the entire assembly.

EM: What are the parties like?

M: There are very flamboyant parties of the underground circuit; big productions happening in clubs. I'll leave it at that. It entails lots of wigs, maybe about three-foot tall wigs, and girls—well not so much girls, but guys dressed as girls hanging from ceilings and swings. It's quite a scene. There's a melting pot of cultures that come together during Fashion Week and that's what's so fun about it. You can go anywhere and be entertained, and step into something or a territory that you haven't necessarily been exposed to, and you absorb.

EM: You modeled in the NYC 2000 show.

M: I modeled in that with Jordan Knight from New Kids on the Block.

EM: How did that come about?

M: I don't necessarily understand how that worked. It probably went through either my label or my management company. I didn't have any relationships, one on one, back then. That was when my first album came out. I was thrilled. I'd never modeled in a fashion show before and I was a little nervous.

EM: More nervous than singing in front of thousands of people?

M: Yeah, you never know if you're doing something right that you've not experienced before or practiced. And you're around all these girls that look a little different—well, *a lot* different in body type. I'm 5'5''. Back then I was wondering, "Does anyone know who I am, or should I even be doing this?" I was insecure.

EM: But I'm sure it was so much fun.

M: Yes it was. All of that prep, you know, you spend hours and hours and days, even months, laying out your designs. It may even be a year to develop your collection, and then months of preparation regarding the theme and color scheme, as well as how the makeup and hair will look. It's almost like planning a wedding. And then the fashion show is about ten minutes. It may go overtime or start an hour late, but it's a ten-minute show usually.

I think people would be surprised by what really goes

into everything. You see ten minutes of a display but you don't realize how much work and planning it all entails. It's like a production, a movie, and there's quite a lot of staff involved, and hiring models behind the scenes and making sure everyone is on time from their last fashion show. I wonder how they schedule that and how they select their models because there are several of the same models in other designers' shows all week.

EM: Is there a favorite collection you've seen over the years?

M: There was a particular show where I got the idea of making leg warmers out of fabrics and putting them over shoes, and it gave the illusion that you were rocking these fabulous boots. So, I started making these leg warmers, with a metallic look, and sewing them myself. People would ask me all the time, "Where did you get those boots from? I've never seen anything like that before." I would lift up the leg warmer and there was just a heel. You can do so many cool things. I learned that from Fashion Week.

FRESH FACES

DOUTZEN KROES

FROM: FRIESLAND, THE NETHERLANDS
HEIGHT: 5'10" | HAIR: BLONDE | EYES: BLUE

JAUNEL MCKENZIE

FROM: KINGSTON, JAMAICA | HEIGHT: 5'10"
HAIR: BROWN | EYES: BROWN

THE SCENE

★ Francisco Costa stepped into the spotlight this season when he took over as creative director for the Calvin Klein collection.

★ Michael Vollbracht debuted as head designer at Bill Blass.

★ Cindy Crawford made a rare runway appearance when she walked for Esteban Cortázar. Crawford loved the crystal dress she wore in the show, although it was extremely heavy.

★ Eight-year-old Evie Goodman Gimbel, daughter of former model and *Vogue* fashion director Tonne Goodman stole the show at Anna Sui. From her seat (the lap of Paul Cavaco) the little girl cheerfully waved to all the models as they walked by. She enchanted the crowd and the models, too.

★ Hard to believe that former model Brooke Shields had not attended a first fashion show until Spring 2004. Shields attended the Michael Kors show, which she loved. She was dressed, appropriately, in head-to-toe Michael Kors.

★ PETA unveiled its fall ad campaign in the tents. The animal rights organization promised Fern Mallis they would not protest any of the shows. In exchange, they were given the chance to get their message across. The ad was shot by Todd Oldham and featured model Fernanda Tavares.

★ Spring 2004 marked Bryan Bradley's first Tuleh show without co-designer Josh Patner.

★ Sixteen designers, including Donna Karan, Carolina Herrera, and Oscar de la Renta, created pants inspired by SpongeBob SquarePants. The clothing was designed to be auctioned off on eBay, with the proceeds benefitting the Elizabeth Glaser Pediatric AIDS Foundation.

★ Natalia Vodianova signed a deal to walk exclusively for Calvin Klein this season.

★ Beyoncé's presence at the Rosa Cha show started a commotion. The paparazzi were so eager to get a shot of her, they kicked and shoved each other out of the way. Security was called in to control the situation.

★ Marc Jacobs had a pinched nerve in his back and had to make Fashion Week appearances wearing a neck brace.

★ Michael Smaldone debuted as designer for Anne Klein. Smaldone replaced Charles Nolan, who left to campaign for presidential hopeful Howard Dean.

★ The Pierrot show took place on the set of *The Maury Povich Show*. The setting was a fake porn movie, with an appearance by Mimi Rogers.

★ Special Appearances: Pat Cleveland and Karen Bjornson walking for Stephen Burrows.

Karen Bjornson

Pat Cleveland

Francisco Costa

Cindy Crawford

Natalia Vodianova

Pierrot

FALL/WINTER
2004
A FEMININE SEASON

PRESENTED FEBRUARY 6–13, 2004

TRENDS:
SECRETARY CHIC

FALL 2004 PRESENTED a tongue-in-cheek take on "demure"/"appropriate" style. Maggie Gyllenhaal made a big splash wearing the style in the 2002 film *Secretary*.

Behnaz Sarafpour

Marc Jacobs, model: Gisele Bündchen

TWEED

TWEED, A FALL staple, hit its heyday again this season with references to the classic Chanel suit. Tweed was also big in coats and pants.

Tuleh

Marc Jacobs, model: Gisele Bündchen

PLEATS

FROM SHARP TO soft, pleating made its mark in skirts, dresses, and even blouses.

Pierrot's poodles

Big hair at Tuleh

Soft makeup at Behnaz Sarafpour

SNAPPED!

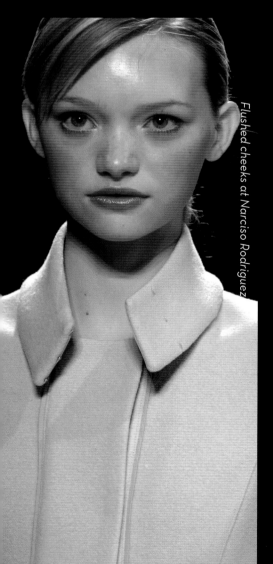

Flushed cheeks at Narciso Rodriguez

Waves at Marc Jacobs

J. Mendel's muff

THE SCENE

★ The event management company 7th on Sixth entered into a multi-year sponsorship deal with camera company Olympus. In addition to being the title sponsor this season, the company also sponsored the shows of Proenza Schouler and Esteban Cortázar.

★ Olympus Fashion Week got started with a ribbon-cutting ceremony with Mayor Michael Bloomberg, Kenneth Cole, and Thom Filicia. Filicia, best known for the Bravo series *Queer Eye for the Straight Guy*, was brought in this season as design director, and given the job of making over the interior of the tents.

★ Photographers were given a treat due to the title sponsorship of Olympus. The company provided extra cameras for them to borrow, iMac stations to work at, and their own lounge.

Theodora and Alexandra Richards

Nanette Lepore

CLAUDIA MASON

op model Claudia Mason has walked the runway for designers such as Isaac Mizrahi, Gianni Versace, Karl Lagerfeld, and Valentino. Also an actress, Mason appeared onstage in Tennessee Williams's *Orpheus Descending*, as well as on television with roles in *How I Met Your Mother* and *CSI: NY*.

EILA MELL: How did you start modeling?

CLAUDIA MASON: I was discovered in Tower Records on the Upper West Side of New York, where I was born and raised. I was there shopping with a friend. I was thirteen and 5'10''. This modeling agent came up to me. She said she normally didn't look for tall girls, because she was in the petite division of Elite, but she wanted me to come in. I went with my dad. I started booking jobs right away, and such amazing jobs. I was able to work with Steven Meisel!

EM: What do you attribute your success to?

CM: Timing—it was a time when my look was in and I think that's really what it comes down to.

EM: What was it like modeling at such a young age?

CM: The agency wanted me to get my GED. My family wasn't interested in that, nor was I. I had the chance to work with Richard Avedon. Everyone thought it was great, but I was crying with my mom because I had to miss school. Thank God I did the Avedon assignment, but when you're fifteen it isn't that cool to hang out with thirty year olds. I didn't think it was that exciting.

EM: Did adults in the industry treat you as a kid or as a peer?

CM: Certain adults would treat me in a more adult way and others would treat me as a kid. It's hard for the teenager to figure out how to act in an adult world, and hard for the adults around them. It can be weird. It's wonderful too though.

EM: Is hair and makeup fun?

CM: Hair and makeup is fun for a show. When you have eight a day it's exhausting.

EM: Is it hard to maintain your weight?

CM: A model is like an athlete. You have to be in top form, especially for the season which is three cities, sometimes four—hopefully doing it healthily and not on drugs. It takes a lot. I think the general idea is models have it so easy, but we do eight shows a day and fittings. You have to be "on," like a performer, and present yourself. It's not just the look—you're performing with your entire self.

EM: When you started the sample size was six, but it's gotten smaller over the years.

CM: The sample sizes were never really sixes. They may have been labeled six, but they were more like four. I think it's always going to be about being a coat hanger. A lot of people are naturally thin. Of course it's an issue, but honestly I don't see any difference in how it is now and how it was ten or fifteen years ago.

EM: You're also an actress and got great reviews starring in the Tennessee Williams play *Orpheus Descending*.

CM: That was such a great experience, it was my dream role.

NEW
ON THE
SCENE

MENICHETTI

Designer Roberto Menichetti's first collection was designed to meet the needs of a new generation. He showed enormous versatility, as he presented clothes that ran the gamut from sweats to eveningwear.

THAKOON

Twenty-nine-year-old Thakoon Panichgul's debut collection was a ten-piece presentation showing metallic taffeta skirts, ribbon-tie jackets, and beige separates.

FRESH FACES

CAMERON RUSSELL

FROM: CAMBRIDGE, MASSACHUSETTS
HEIGHT: 5'9" | HAIR: BROWN | EYES:
BROWN

NATASHA POLY

FROM: PERM, RUSSIA | HEIGHT: 5'10"
HAIR: BLONDE | EYES: GREEN

CINTIA DICKER

FROM: CAMPO BORN, RIO GRANDE DO SUL, BRAZIL
HEIGHT: 5'10" | HAIR: RED | EYES: BLUE

ARIEL FOXMAN

Ariel Foxman is the managing editor of *InStyle* magazine. Foxman came to the publication in 1999. He was also editor in chief of the men's magazine *Cargo*. Foxman made a cameo appearance as himself in a 2008 episode of *Gossip Girl*.

EILA MELL: How does New York Fashion Week influence what you do at *InStyle*?

ARIEL FOXMAN: It's the start to every fashion season and so it begins to set the tone for the trends and news we'll be prioritizing and presenting to our audience in the coming months. New York is always such a great way to reconnect with colleagues and industry friends whom you see every day for weeks during show season, but then don't have the opportunity to see once show season is through.

EM: How are celebrities important to the fashion industry?

AF: Celebrities are still the most photographed people at any fashion show, so their presence and excitement for a particular designer can bring a spotlight to a house, label, or brand that might not necessarily have it, or at the level they deserve. Celebrities are also first to wear many of the trends (fashion, hair, and beauty) that we see on the runway; so the consumer looks to celebrities to see how trends translate off the runway and into real life.

EM: What was the first show you ever attended at NY Fashion Week?

AF: My first show was Kenneth Cole, when I was covering menswear while editor in chief of *Cargo*. It was thrilling. Kenneth Cole's shows are notoriously big in scale and clever in presentation so it made a very strong first impression.

EM: Women's fashion dominates the runways. Would you say menswear is well represented?

AF: It's represented in a way that integrates itself within the context of women's Fashion Week. There is no separate men's Fashion Week calendar in New York, like there is in other cities. Still, for the retailers and editors that work in men's fashion, New York shows do what they need to do and have a life of their own.

EM: Any favorite memories from the tents?

AF: Sitting next to Kathy Griffin at Isaac Mizrahi. The laughs were coming out faster than the looks.

Valentina Zelyaeva and Ralph Lauren

SNAPPED!

Rebecca Taylor

Tara Subkoff

SPRING/SUMMER

2005

A CLASSIC SEASON

PRESENTED SEPTEMBER 8–15, 2004

TRENDS:
AMERICAN WEST

DESIGNERS WERE INSPIRED
by classic Americana, from fringe details to denim to gingham prints.

Matthew Williamson

Marc Jacobs

FLORALS

A FRESH SPIN on the classic spring motif was seen on runways.

Zac Posen, model: Jessica Stam

Proenza Schouler

VOLUME

THE PLAY OF shape on the body was emphasized in Spring 2005 collections. Designers typically select an area to focus volume on; perhaps on a sleeve, a skirt, or even trousers. The tulip shape, a classic take on volume, saw a resurgence.

OTHER HIGHLIGHTS

Accessories at Michael Kors

Zac Posen's ponytails

Dewy at Calvin Klein Collection

Tommy Hilfiger's necklaces, model: Erin Wasson

Stephen Burrows updo

THE SCENE

★ Marc Jacobs and Anna Sui included the line "Leonard Peltier is Innocent" in their show's notes. In doing so they were supporting fellow designer Vivienne Westwood, who was working to free Peltier. The Native American Peltier had been convicted and sentenced to two consecutive life terms for the murder of two FBI agents, Jack R. Coler and Ronald A. Williams, in a 1975 shootout on the Pine Ridge Indian Reservation. Many consider the proceedings that led to his conviction to have been unfair. The 1992 film *Incident at Oglala* documents Peltier's case.

★ In a booth backstage at the tents, Miriam Maltagliata set up a space to teach those interested in learning how to knit.

★ Miguel Adrover's show in Sarah D. Roosevelt Park ended with the designer in a T-shirt that read "Anyone See a Backer?" Adrover referred to this show as a battle for retail relevance and survival.

★ Illusionist David Blaine casually entertained designer Jennifer Nicholson's audience while waiting for her show to start. Looking on was Nicholson's father, Jack.

★ John Demsey, of MAC cosmetics, presented the company's first ever Star of the Week award to Naomi Campbell.

★ Gottex designer Gideon Oberson showed a one-of-a-kind swimsuit worth $18 million in diamonds. The suit sported approximately two hundred diamonds including a 103-carat pear-shaped diamond.

★ Keith Richards was applauded by the audience of Stephen Burrows's show, where he watched his daughter, Alexandra, model. Due to some seating snafu Richards was in the wrong seat, which caused *Elle* editor Nicole Phelps to have to sit on coworker Anne Slowey's lap.

★ Gen Art, an organization to support the next generation of emerging talent, celebrated their tenth anniversary.

★ Katie Couric, Iman, Mayor Bloomberg, and others were on hand at the tents to introduce "Be Seen, Be Screened," a colon cancer screening initiative. The effort was intended to raise awareness and encourage early screenings. Designer Carmen Marc Valvo, a survivor of the disease, was also there and spoke to the crowd about his experience. Olympus, Fashion Week's title sponsor, unveiled designer items that would be auctioned off on eBay to benefit the National Colorectal Cancer Research Alliance.

★ Special appearance: Farrah Fawcett walking for Yeohlee

★ Designer Alice Roi had no idea how her runway show would end. Unbeknownst to Roi, her boyfriend, Narc Beckman, arranged for her models to hold up signs which read, "Will You Marry Me?" The emotional moment concluded with Roi saying yes.

KATHERINE ENSSLEN

Katherine Ensslen is the Director of Makeup Artistry and Fashion Production for MAC Cosmetics. Throughout her career, Ensslen has also produced theatrical productions, sporting events, music festivals, and diplomatic dinners.

EILA MELL: What does your job at MAC entail?

KATHERINE ENSSLEN: I do all the fashion sponsorships for MAC Cosmetics worldwide. We participate in about twenty-three different Fashion Weeks worldwide. I coordinate and schedule all of our teams for all of the shows we support. I also do all the contracts and deal with the agents and the key makeup artists. At the shows I go backstage and help coordinate models; make sure everyone gets their hair and makeup done. It sounds simple but it's not. It usually means a lot of running around, pulling models, finding out who is coming late, finding out from the front-of-house people when the show's actually going to happen (not just scheduled to happen).

EM: When did MAC become involved with the shows?

KE: We signed on in about 1995. February 2009 was the last official sponsorship at the tents. We decided to change our positioning with being at Bryant Park and running our own space at Milk Studios.

EM: Is models arriving late a typical problem?

KE: There are always a ton of late girls. Notoriously, someone's going to come with the complete opposite of what you want them to have. They'll have giant hair and glitter all over them when you're doing straight hair and no makeup. If you have ten or twenty girls for a show, usually three or four come screaming late, sometimes after the show is officially set to start. You're never quite sure if you're going to get it done.

EM: Has it ever not gotten done?

KE: At show time if so and so isn't here, they'll see if her outfit fits another girl, maybe the order has to change, even after someone has spent an excruciating amount of time planning. Or an outfit just won't go out which is even more painful. It makes everyone crazy.

EM: How do the designers and makeup artists arrive at the look for the show?

KE: Usually a couple of days before the show there's what they call hair and makeup tests. At that point the person who's going to be designing the look for the hair and the person who's designing the look for the makeup meet with the designer, stylist, and a model. They try some ideas, discuss what they're thinking, and get on the same page.

EM: How has beauty in New York Fashion Week evolved over the years?

KE: The mid 1990s was the beginning of people using makeup artists. Before that a lot of models did their own makeup. As it started to evolve you wanted a higher level of precision or a more specified look.

EM: How many makeup artists make up a team?

KE: Usually you have one artist for every two models at a show. If there are twenty models, we have a key person and probably nine assistants. The key person does a demonstration of what the look is, step by step, because these people have never seen it before. Then everyone goes away and does their models and then they show them to the key to get approved.

EM: Is there a New York look?

KE: I think there's a more sophisticated palette that happens. I think that New York is a consumer-based city, London has more artistry, and Paris has more whimsy. On the average, in New York people want something you can relate to. They don't want over-drawn eyebrows or overly exaggerated things.

EM: What is new, makeup-wise?

KE: It's about the technology of the products. There's always going to be red lips, but the question for the highly educated beauty consumer and journalist is about the technology of it and the application. Does it feel very precise, glamorous, and luxurious or is it fun and fanciful?

EM: What do you think people should know about New York Fashion Week?

KE: It's a very professional program. These are top-notch professional people who do this for a living. It's not a lark for them. When you're working with them you get quality product and quality relationships. It's great to work with the crème de la crème of any industry and New York Fashion Week has a super high tier of people producing.

NEW ON THE SCENE

COSTELLO TAGLIAPIETRA

Jeffrey Costello and Robert Tagliapietra met in 1994. Coincidentally, both men had been introduced to fashion by their grandmothers, who both had worked for designer Norman Norell in the 1960s. Ten years after meeting they presented their first collection at New York Fashion Week.

FRESH
FACES

NOAH MILLS

FROM: BALTIMORE, MARYLAND | HEIGHT: 6'2" | HAIR: BROWN | EYES: BROWN

LARS BURMEISTER

FROM: HAMBURG, GERMANY | HEIGHT: 6'1" | HAIR: BROWN | EYES: BLUE

Jennifer and Jack Nicholson

Catherine Malandrino

Miho Aoki and Thuy Pham with models

SNAPPED!

Gottex's $18 million-dollar swimsuit

Farrah Fawcett at Yeohlee

Narciso Rodriguez, model: Bianca Balti

FALL/WINTER
2005
SERIOUS FASHION

PRESENTED FEBRUARY 4-11, 2005

TRENDS: RUSSIA

THE RUSSIAN TREND of Fall 2005 featured fur hats and embroidered details. This look had been made famous in fashion circles by Yves Saint Laurent in the 1970s.

Nanette Lepore

Anna Sui, model: Naomi Campbell

Custo Barcelona

ANTI-FASHION

A LITTLE GOTH, a little of Mary-Kate and Ashley Olsen, and a lot of black. The idea was not to be attractive or sexy—intellectualism reigned.

Ralph Lauren

Kenneth Cole

CAREER DRESSING

THIS LOOK, THE antithesis of anti-fashion, also made it to the runways this season. It is the stuff that establishments are made of.

OTHER HIGHLIGHTS

Heatherette's spider

Ralph Lauren's aviators

Proenza Schouler's dress

THE SCENE

★ Kai Kuhne announced his departure from the design quartet As Four.

★ Melania Trump was awarded MAC's Star of the Week Award.

★ Unbelievably, André Leon Talley was denied entrance to the Baby Phat show. After Talley was told to wait in line he left and went to Zac Posen's showroom instead for a peek at the designer's collection.

★ Isabella Rossellini had the pleasure of watching her daughter Elettra Wiedemann walk a runway for the first time at Catherine Malandrino's show. Although Wiedemann had walked before, she was not yet ready for her mother to see her until this particular show.

★ The crowd gathered at the Marc Jacobs show grew impatient after ninety minutes of waiting for the show to start. At around 10:30 PM, Beyoncé came out from backstage and was treated to a round of boos from the audience, who thought she was the reason for the long delay. It was explained that the real reason was that the clothes had arrived late. A couple of days later, marcjacobs.com had a notice reading: "The Marc Jacobs Spring-Summer 2006 collection will be held Sept. 12th at 9:00 PM. Please be advised the show is running approximately 1½ hours late. Please check here for monthly updates." Marc Jacobs International president Robert Duffy explained that the company was truly sorry about the delay, and the joke on the website was intended to lighten everyone's mood.

★ Dennis Rodman showed up at the tents as a spokesperson for PETA. Rodman, who famously sported many tattoos, posed nude for the organization's campaign with the tag line "Think Ink, Not Mink."

★ Photographer Timothy Greenfield-Sanders took portraits of Beyoncé, Sarah Ferguson, Laura Bush, Heidi Klum, Carolina Herrera, Betsey Johnson, and others in a booth erected by Olympus.

★ Special appearances: Richie Rich walking for B-Rude; Harry Belafonte walking for Kenneth Cole

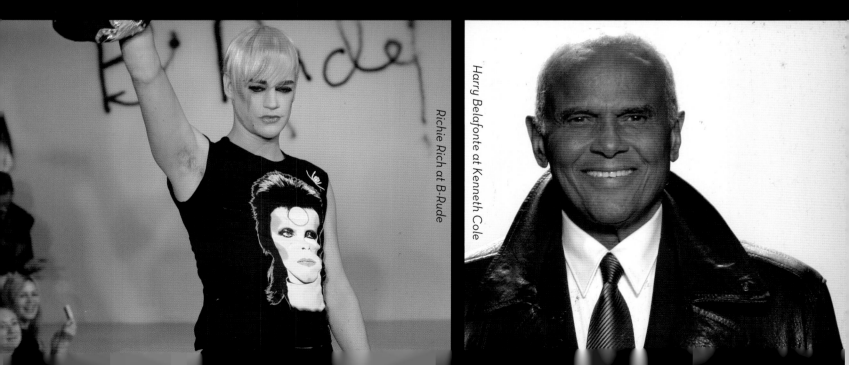

Richie Rich at B-Rude

Harry Belafonte at Kenneth Cole

KARA SAUN

Kara Saun was on season one of the hit series *Project Runway*. Since then she has appeared on E!, Style Network, Bravo, and TV Guide Channel. Saun is a very busy costume designer, with credits such as *Eve*, *What I Like about You*, and *Malcolm & Eddie*.

EILA MELL: Was *Project Runway* the first time you showed at New York Fashion Week?

KARA SAUN: Other than the renegade fashion show I staged in 1994, yes. What a week it was. Just think, on top of the normal excitement that swirls around you during Fashion Week, I also was contending with the fact that I was in the midst of a competition that was being televised for the world to see and I couldn't wait! It had been a long road to the *Project Runway* finale.

Born in Germany, I was an air force brat who had traveled the world and landed in South Carolina as my final destination. A self-taught designer, I would literally sew night and day throughout my high school years and continued to during my years at Rutgers University in New Jersey. I remember being at Rutgers and hopping the train to New York to sell my clothes to boutiques. My first order came from a store in Soho called La Rue de Rêves. Shortly after my renegade fashion show I received an amazing opportunity in a job as assistant costumer in Los Angeles. I didn't spend too much time as an assistant. I quickly moved up to costume designer and spent the next ten years building my career in entertainment. I had already designed for the shows *Eve* and *The Queen Latifah Show* by the time another great opportunity came—*Project Runway*. It was a perfect gift from God, literally. It fell from the sky just at the right time and once again I was off to New York for

the next big adventure.

EM: Can you tell me about the renegade show you staged?

KS: I was in New York. Fashion Week was coming. I thought, "What can I do? No one knows who I am." Back then in Europe they had these renegade fashion shows where you would just crash a fashion show with one of your own. I decided to have my own renegade show. First I needed models, so I called some that I had worked with. Then I got my hairstylist friend and makeup artist friend. I don't know where I got the money from, but I hired two limousines. I told everybody what we were going to do. They thought I was crazy.

We pull up in front of Calvin Klein's show. We say a prayer before we get out. There were crowds outside the show waiting to get in. There were editors, buyers, fashionistas. The girls started modeling and everybody just stopped and looked. Next thing I know I was interviewed by *The New York Times*. We made the cover of the *Village Voice*. Everybody was talking about it. Exactly ten years later I was doing *Project Runway*. My second day there I met Tim Gunn. He said, "Kara Saun, I know who you are. I remember your renegade fashion show ten years ago. Everybody at Parsons was talking about it. You showed them what it took to have guts in fashion."

EM: Do you think as a woman you have an advantage as a designer?

KS: Absolutely. I think for the type of design I do and for my Red Carpet line, I create with all the elements I love as a woman, involving sexy yet sophisticated cuts, absolutely gorgeous materials, intricate detailing, and amazing construction.

EM: What's the main difference between designing for a particular television show and designing a collection?

KS: I absolutely love costume design. I love the creative process. I love the fast pace—I may have three days to turn around a hundred costumes for a particular show and it all has to look amazing. I love taking a director or producer's vision and giving them something they didn't even know existed. When designing for television there are a number of things to consider, from the talent, to the wishes of the network, director and producers, to the theme and script. Also, the fact that millions of people each week will be inspired by what you create and put on the air.

When I'm designing my own line, on the other hand, I really only answer to myself. I have to create what I want and what I love. The creative process starts with me and where I find my inspiration.

EM: What would people be surprised to know about New York Fashion Week?

KS: I think that people would be surprised at the massive adrenaline rush one gets at the realization that the past four or five months of no sleep, non-stop designing, construction, and reworking culminates in a mere ten or fifteen minutes on the runway.

CHILD MAGAZINE SHOW

CHILD MAGAZINE HELD its first ever children's fashion show at the Bryant Park tents on February 7, 2005.

NEW
ON THE
SCENE

B-Rude

3.1 PHILLIP LIM

At the suggestion of friend Wen Zhou, Phillip Lim created his own label. Less than a year later, 3.1 Phillip Lim premiered at New York Fashion Week to rave reviews.

B-RUDE

Debbie Harry, Rose McGowan, and others gathered at the Maritime Hotel to see the debut of B-Rude, the new line by 1980s icon Boy George.

FRESH FACES

MIRANDA KERR

FROM: SYDNEY, AUSTRALIA | HEIGHT: 5'9"
HAIR: BROWN | EYES: BLUE

HYE PARK

FROM: SEOUL, SOUTH KOREA | HEIGHT: 5'9"
HAIR: BLACK | EYES: BROWN

PAUL WILMOT

Paul Wilmot is a managing partner of Paul Wilmot Communications. Prior to launching the company with partners Ridgely Brooks and Stormy Stokes, Wilmot was the Senior Vice President for Public Relations and Communications at Calvin Klein. He was later brought on to *Vogue* as Director of Public Relations and Communications.

EILA MELL: How has New York Fashion Week evolved since it started?

PAUL WILMOT: The biggest changes are the incredible increases in the number of international publications that attend, and of course the Internet and digital presence that exists now. Some of the bloggers have up to 60 million hits a month. Those numbers and that power are irrefutable.

EM: What are the weeks leading up to Fashion Week like at your office?

PW: It starts slowly and finishes fast here. They start sending out the invitations and getting the seating charts ready. Then there is the frenzy at the end to make sure that everyone attending whatever we are doing is accounted for, and that all the press interviews with our designers have been confirmed.

EM: Your clients include some of the most established designers in the industry, like Oscar de la Renta, as well as newer designers. What is the difference in your working relationships?

PW: Of course working with a master like Oscar is a humbling privilege as he is unerring in his ability to get it just right season after season. However, working with some of the newer designers can be gratifying too, as we see them bloom and get better with each passing season.

EM: How is your job different with new designers?

PW: The new designers learn how to get the clothes ready on time, how to attract the important editors and retailers, and how to work with stylists to make sure the line is tuned up perfectly.

EM: What goes into the decision for a designer to have a presentation rather than a runway show?

PW: Runway or presentation varies from designer to designer. We encourage newer ones to do presentations as there are so many shows for the editors and stores to attend and the two-hour timeframe of the presentation ensures that all who need to see the clothes can.

EM: What are some of your favorite moments from the tents?

PW: I just remember the Bryant Park tents growing year after year. I remember when Mayor Giuliani came to do a press visit it was a big deal. In the years that followed everyone seems to have made their way there at one time or another.

EM: What is your favorite part of NY Fashion Week?

PW: Seeing the collections—I never get tired of that, and I also enjoy the quiet dinners that take place during the week. It is so nice to catch up with out of towners one might only see a couple of times a year.

EM: What would people be surprised to know about New York Fashion Week?

PW: That it is not all glamour by any means, and a lot of hard work.

Tori Spelling

Ralph Lauren with family in background

SNAPPED!

Beyoncé, Mark Jacobs, and Jay-Z

Jennifer Nicholson

SPRING/SUMMER
2006
A ROMANTIC SEASON
PRESENTED SEPTEMBER 9–16, 2005

TRENDS:
SHEER

DESIGNERS PLAYED WITH the use of illusion to illustrate a new sex appeal for Spring 2006.

Morgane Le Fay

Jennifer Nicholson

ROMANCE

ROMANCE WAS IN the air this season. Soft dresses made a comeback.

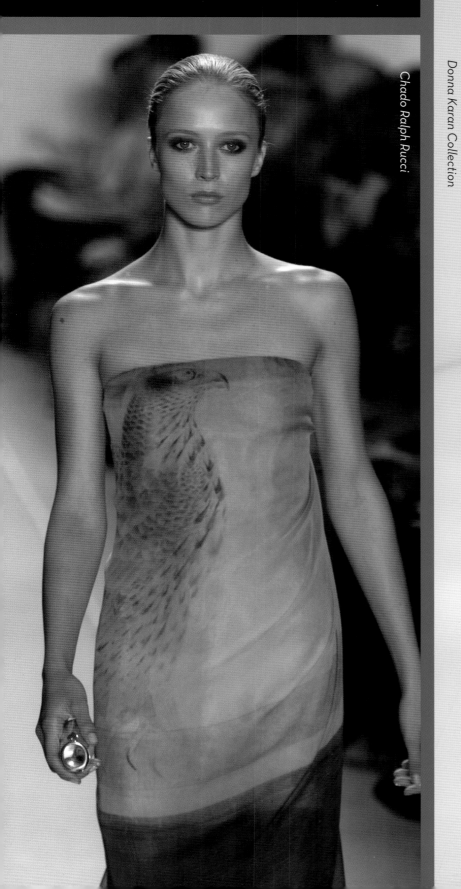

ART

THE INFLUENCE OF fine artists was felt on the Spring/Summer 2006 runways.

Chado Ralph Rucci

Donna Karan Collection

OTHER HIGHLIGHTS

Lined eyes at Donna Karan Collection

Heatherette's updo

Marc Jacobs bag

Heatherette's bow

Michael Kors' tans

THE SCENE

★ Fashion Week was kicked off this season by Condé Nast's Fashion Rocks concert. Held at Radio City Music Hall, the concert was hosted by Sugar Ray's Mark McGrath. Actress Poppy Montgomery, David Bowie, Destiny's Child, Rob Thomas, Joss Stone, Billy Idol, Shakira, and Alicia Keys were among the artists who performed. Proceeds from the event went to Hurricane Katrina relief efforts. The concert was shown on television the following night.

★ Calvin Klein's show at Milk Studios was hot. The air conditioning was out of service.

★ Marc Jacobs' show featured a marching band from Penn State. The band won over the crowd with their interpretation of Nirvana's "Smells Like Teen Spirit."

★ Several guests of Diane von Furstenberg's show were injured when a rack of stage lights fell from above while models were on the runway. Hilary Alexander, a reporter for London's *Daily Telegraph* was taken out on a stretcher. *The Daily*'s Karl Treacy sustained a head injury, and *Teen Vogue*'s Amy Astley was cut on her back. A shaken von Fürstenberg followed up with all the injured parties and was relieved to learn that no one was seriously hurt. She also sent flowers and apologized to them all.

★ Tommy Hilfiger's show celebrated the designer's twentieth year in fashion. His show began with a video presentation commemorating his career.

★ Kimora Lee's Baby Phat show was held at New York's iconic Radio City Music Hall.

★ Lillian Bassmon attended Joanna Mastroianni's show. It was the famed fashion photographer's first show in almost sixty years.

★ Models Caroline Trentini, Cintia Dicker, and Heather Marks were in a car accident just before they were supposed to walk in the Badgley Mischka show. They were uninjured, and made it to the show.

★ Special appearances: Janice Dickinson walking for B-Rude; Nicky Hilton, Amanda Lepore, and Kelly Osbourne walking for Heatherette.

Kenneth Cole

The Penn State marching band at Marc Jacobs

FASHION FOR RELIEF

IN AUGUST OF 2005, Hurricane Katrina hit the Gulf coast region of the country. It was one of the deadliest hurricanes in recorded history, with the loss of almost two thousand lives. Total property damage was estimated at $81 billion.

    Among the people who wanted to help was Naomi Campbell. She offered her modeling services to any New York designer at September's New York Fashion Week on the condition that they would donate her entire pricey fee to aid the victims. Campbell went one step further and in addition took on the Herculean task of organizing the charity show Fashion for Relief in just two weeks. Campbell reached out to her friends in fashion and entertainment and got major celebrities to walk the runway. Tickets went on sale to the general public for $100 a piece. Campbell's efforts were successful, as nearly a thousand people attended the show and donated a great deal of money to those in need.

Nicole Richie

Beyoncé

Tyson Beckford

Lydia Hearst

Naomi Campbell

Kelly Osbourne

NEW ON THE SCENE

Brian Reyes

L.A.M.B.

L.A.M.B.

Rocker Gwen Stefani referenced *The Sound of Music*, *Rasta*, Orange County chola girls, and *The Great Gatsby* for her first runway show.

BRIAN REYES

Twenty-four-year-old Brian Reyes had strong buzz for his first collection as *The New York Times* had already been a supporter of his. The self-taught designer previously worked at Ralph Lauren, Michael Kors, and Oscar de la Renta.

ROBERT VERDI

Robert Verdi is a stylist known for his television appearances in which he shares his expertise on fashion and interior design. He has worked with many celebrities as a style expert including Hugh Jackman, Eva Longoria, Mariska Hargitay, Sandra Bernhard, and Bobby Flay. Robert co-created and co-hosted *Full Frontal Fashion* on Metro TV. He served as host for *Surprise by Design* and *Fashion Police*. He was a judge on *She's Got the Look* and star of his own reality series, *The Robert Verdi Show*.

EILA MELL: What were some of your early Bryant Park experiences like?

ROBERT VERDI: I was so concerned with getting into the shows that it didn't matter what show I got into. I remember the first show that made me feel like I had arrived in Oz was Isaac Mizrahi's—a show called Metamorphoses. It was one of those shows that, for whatever reason, made a dent in my mind that has stayed forever. He took you through a tour of what's going on in his mind. He has a really interesting sense of wonder about the world. He creates all of these wonderful vignettes; they're moments forever gone, experienced by the few who were there. To me, that's what those tents were able to do. The tents were essentially Oz for many people.

EM: How do fashion shows impact your job as a stylist?

RV: It's interesting. With the exception of the men's shows, I'm really good at disconnecting my own tastes. The idea is to get inside your clients' heads, and understand what they are trying to accomplish with their public image. I think what people take for granted is what a stylist really has to do. It's more than just being the person who zips the dress. In many ways you're part art dealer, because there are only so many dresses per season. You have to leverage your relationships and the weight of your celebrity. You're essentially bidding on those dresses. You also want your clients to lead the trends based on what you send down the runway. You want them to be the first, so that they're thought of as a trendsetter.

EM: So a celebrity's clothing is part of their overall image?

RV: Take Oprah. We've never thought of her as a fashion icon even though she wears some incredibly fabulous things. But we don't address her style because she speaks to us every day. She has a conversation with the nation, with the world. Celebrities don't. Their dialogue is what they're wearing. It influences our opinions about them. Britney with flip-flops or barefoot, shaved head in a parking lot, tells us a different story than Britney in some fabulous little dress performing in Vegas. That's how people decide if they like a celebrity.

EM: There are so many things that people don't realize that goes into choosing a dress.

RV: There's a lot to think about. Someone like Eva Longoria, part of the ensemble cast of *Desperate Housewives*—if she's not nominated and someone else is, and she goes with too big of a fashion statement it'll look like she's trying to steal the show. You're always dealing with psychological issues. Eva was named *Maxim*'s Sexiest Woman two years in a row. At the time it was colliding with awards season. I told her that she had to scale it back because she would lose her female fan base if all she appeared to be was some hot bitch who steals their husbands. So we had to do something pretty, but not really sexy. I put her in a circle skirt, sweetheart neckline—a Grace Kelly-looking thing. So that's what you're doing as a stylist. And you're always looking to add another level, a new dimension to your client's public image.

EM: Is it important that your clients attend Fashion Week?

RV: I have a rule: if you don't have a relationship with that designer, you shouldn't be at their show. Kathy Griffin's gone to Badgley Mischka because she's worn Badgley Mischka. There are some companies that just invite because they want the frenzy in the front row. I'll decline it and tell the client that it looks gratuitous, like they're getting paid.

EM: How important are trends for the average person?

RV: I'm not concerned with trends. I think that women need to be informed about what's out there, and then use whatever skills they've honed to determine which of those things can make their wardrobe exciting. The reality is that you don't get rid of your entire wardrobe every season and buy a new one. You're constantly adding pieces to update what you already have. You use any trend that accentuates what you love about yourself, whether it's your waist or you've got great boobs. If you're barrel shaped, when Tory Burch did her tunic you should have been all over that shit! And you should have a bunch of them in your wardrobe because you're going to be able to use them forever, and feel great in them. They might not be on trend, but you'll be okay. And you'll add to that which becomes a wardrobe staple for you. All trends that work for you become a wardrobe staple. Then the next season you wear that tunic in a different way, with Louboutins, a bare leg, ballet flat; whatever is in.

EM: What's the most fun part of Fashion Week?

RV: Really as a fashion lover, the most fun is when you're in the room for that watershed moment. That's why people travel from around the world. They want to be there when there's a cultural shift; when someone figures out what later seems really obvious, that this thing was missing and could create great commerce. It's a watershed moment, not just for fashion. It's a cultural shift. Fashion records our culture.

Like Donna Karan in the 1980s, with the crepe drape. And all those bodysuits she did. She all of the sudden figured that women wanted to look sexy. Women are strong and tough and empowered and are in the work-place and don't have to sacrifice their femininity. Each time you walk into a show it's like buying a scratch-and-win ticket, because you might be there when something really great happens.

EM: Any favorite moments from Bryant Park?

RV: Standing in line at the very first fashion season, when the tents were new. They hadn't yet established a system where the real establishment would move seamlessly into the tents. I was standing next to Polly Mellen, who's an icon. That couldn't happen today, because she'd be swept straight into the tents.

I remember Todd Oldham's show with Linda and Naomi and Christy and Cindy.

Getting a front-row seat at the Michael Kors show for the first time because I used to crash the show and then jump into the front row.

EM: What was it like working on *Full Frontal Fashion*?

RV: Judy Licht concocted the program. It was a non-stop fashion event. At first we weren't getting invited to anything. Then Donna Karan invited us to cover her show. By the third day we were invited to everything. I remember interviewing Carolina Herrera for the first time. That was a big moment. I couldn't even ask questions, my hand was shaking! She is beyond lovely. She's polished and charming and so well bred.

EM: Do you think people have misconceptions about the fashion industry?

RV: I think the industry's often chided as being superficial, but there is great artistry in fashion. With that comes a lot of responsibility to a lot of people who work in the garment center. Yes, there's this happening in New York City which is called Fashion Week. People forget that the UPS man who's delivering your orders from J Crew is tied to the Fashion Week industry. So are all the employees that are servicing retailers, the contractors that build stores, anybody who's had a job that is in any way inside the fashion ecosystem. It doesn't have to be a job about the runway. Your dry cleaner has a fashion job. People forget how deep it is. It's not all about the runway and the editors. It's unfortunate that people don't realize how valuable the industry is.

Donna Karan Collection, model: Jessica Stam

FALL/WINTER
2006
A SEASON OF BLACK
PRESENTED FEBRUARY 3–10, 2006

TRENDS:
FUR

PETA'S CRIES WERE heard, although not completely for Fall 2006. Show goers saw a mix of fur, both faux and real, and even in colors.

Chado Ralph Rucci

Heatherette

LAYERING

DESIGNERS GAVE MANY options for head-to-toe layering of clothing and accessories.

BLACK

AS A RULE, black is always a fashion statement, but this season it dominated in a way that made retailers scream. This trend extended throughout Milan and Paris.

Karl Lagerfeld

Ralph Lauren

Bill Blass

Luca Luca's straight hair

OTHER HIGHLIGHTS

Bright lip color at Donna Karan Collection

Jeremy Scott's hamburger and french fries

THE SCENE

German designer Karl Lagerfeld showed his self-titled line in New York for the first time. Lagerfeld's venue of choice was a Chelsea ballet studio.

Marc Jacobs International president, Robert Duffy, announced ahead of time that the Marc Jacobs show, scheduled for 8 PM, would not start before 9:30. He and Jacobs found out that a delivery of shoes for the show was coming later than expected, causing the inevitable delay. Duffy wanted people to know ahead of time, so they could show up later and avoid a long wait that had ruffled feathers in prior seasons.

As Four went on with the show minus designer Kai Kuhne. Kuhne showed under his own label, Myself, while his former design partners renamed their line threeASFOUR.

Chaiken designer Julie Chaiken had a very good reason for missing her own show. She had recently given birth to a baby boy. Jeff Mahshie, the company's creative director, kept things running smoothly.

A crowd showed up to see Mary J. Blige perform at Catherine Malandrino's show at the Roseland Ballroom.

The thirty-four-year-old cashmere company Malo had its first ever New York show. The company's CEO, Stefano Ferro, said that the move from Milan was made to give the label greater exposure.

Natalia Vodianova was unable to walk the runways this season. She was almost eight months pregnant during Fashion Week. However, a seven-months pregnant Karen Elson took to the runway for Marc Jacobs.

Special appearances: Tinsley Mortimer and Amanda Lepore walking for Heatherette

Tinsley Mortimer at Heatherette

Amanda Lepore at Heatherette

Karl Lagerfeld

DANIEL VOSOVIC

Daniel Vosovic's first big exposure to the world was on season two of *Project Runway*. He is the author of the book *Fashion Inside Out*, in which he illustrated the design process from start to finish and conducted interviews with Diane von Furstenberg, Todd Oldham, and Tim Gunn, among others. Daniel launched his own collection in February 2010, a culmination of his signature innovative silhouettes and evocative finesse.

EILA MELL: What did being on *Project Runway* do for your career?

DANIEL VOSOVIC: I was on the show four days after I graduated from college. They don't tell you you're on the show until three days prior and then you have to pack your bags and leave for a month. It moved my career ahead ten years. I knew I wanted to be in this industry when I was seventeen years old. I knew what kind of company I wanted to have. And the show shortened that process. It put me on the radar. I haven't looked back at those photos or watched my season in years. It's funny, as a fashion designer you're taught to look forward. It's so funny that people will still come up to me or write to me. You can tell that the show goes on to international circuits because all of the sudden I'm getting seventy emails from Russia. This thing just keeps having legs, unlike a normal fashion season where as soon as it shows it's over. I'm grateful for it.

EM: So many of the shows were live streamed. What do you think of that?

DV: I loved when Burberry started doing it and they had pre-made some of their jackets. I thought it was an amazing idea. People around the world saw that jacket and could order it right then and there. It's a tricky thing though, because you're completely changing the cycle. A small designer doesn't have the capacity to pre-make a collection. This is my first year. I remember right after I showed a couple of weeks ago I had 327 emails asking where my stuff was sold. In two months are those same people going to be committed? I've started wondering if it's necessary to wait when I know I have people in Moscow, St. Tropez, and Milan we're selling to.

You can try to do it the old way. It's great that Bergdorf's loved our dresses, but at the end of the day there is one Bergdorf's. It's the ivory tower, but a lot of the people who are going to buy my stuff don't have access to it. I'm really trying to grapple with what works for me.

EM: It must be an exciting time.

DV: It's scary and exciting. Luckily, I've had a great opportunity since the show to build my team the proper way.

EM: Do you think too much is expected of new designers?

DV: The learning curve is so fast now. There is a huge amount of pressure for young designers to hit it out of the park not only this time, but the next three times for people to even care. With technology, everyone's a critic now. Look at who's in the front row. Everyone has a blog. Everyone has a voice.

The feedback you get from stores and from editors is, "We like where you're going, but we want to make sure that you can survive,"—meaning, before they invest their publicity, money, and time they want to make sure that you can stand on your own two feet. I did launch a company coming out of a recession. That was a really conscious choice of mine—to make fireworks at a time everyone was cutting back and say, "I'm here. My foundation is solid. Support me; I support you. Let's grow together."

EM: Do you ever encounter any backlash in the industry as a result of being associated with a reality show?

DV: No. For the most part it's opened a lot of doors. I mean, two weeks ago Fern Mallis came to my show and saw me backstage. That connection was originally made from the show. The positive absolutely outweighs the negative, and who knows what my life would be like without it. You probably wouldn't be talking to me.

EM: Was showing with *Project Runway* your first time at Bryant Park?

DV: I came to New York to go to design school, and I cannot tell you how many shows I used to sneak into! My friends and I would go and hang out and bring cameras. It was a fashion parade. The plumage was so colorful and it was so extravagant. It was a lot of fun. Then all of the sudden, there I am. I think I was probably twenty-four. I was having my first show at Bryant Park when literally six months before that I was there "oohing" and "aahing." I couldn't believe I was walking into the tents that I had revered for so long. It was definitely an unforgettable experience.

EM: As a new designer, how involved are you with the running of your company?

DV: Right now I'm involved in every single aspect. I don't know if that's going to change because as things get bigger you have to delegate. But as of right now I have my hand in every single thing that is seen, that's not seen, that goes on in this company. I still pay the bills. I am CFO. I am the designer. I juggle the accounting and PR, the look books. I still Photoshop and clean up the images. And that's why I don't have a TV!

EM: What would people be surprised to know about New York Fashion Week?

DV: I remember the first time I was helping backstage I was shocked to see naked girl upon naked girl and no one batted an eye. Then to see literally six people surround a girl at a time. You have three hair people, and someone's fixing the shoes, and you have no idea what the girl looks like because she has a swarm of people around her. And then they move to the next one, and the next one. I love that. I love looking at this whole gay spray that gets around her.

FRESH FACE

BEHATI PRINSLOO

FROM: GROOTFONTEIN, NAMIBIA
HEIGHT: 5'10" | HAIR: BLONDE | EYES: HAZEL

THE HEART TRUTH FASHION SHOW

BEGINNING IN 2003, once a year celebrities would take to the runway for the Heart Truth fashion show, part of a national campaign sponsored by the National Heart, Lung, and Blood Institute to raise awareness about women's risk of heart disease.

Lindsay Lohan

Thalia

Bebe Neuwirth

Fergie

Debbie Harry

Sheryl Crow

SNAPPED!

Marc Anthony

Patrick McDonald

Mary J. Blige and Catherine Malandrino

Jennifer Lopez and models

Rodarte

SPRING/SUMMER
2007
A LOOSER SEASON
PRESENTED SEPTEMBER 8–15, 2006

TRENDS:
BODY CON

IT WAS EASY to be reminded of Azzedine Alaïa and Helmut Lang, as the contours of the body were highlighted in body con fashion on the runways for Spring 2007.

Rock & Republic

Erin Fetherston

A-LINE

THE SACK DRESS started to emerge as fashionistas loosened up for spring. Styles became more relaxed and a bit bohemian.

THE DANCE TREND was not a literal take on tutus, but rather a feeling of what dancers wore in rehearsal. Sweaters were light, while tulle and netting were soft.

Miss Sixty

Vera Wang

Jeremy Scott

Narciso Rodriguez's makeup

Lined eyes at Rodarte

OTHER HIGHLIGHTS

Ballerina buns at Vera Wang

Flowers at Marc Jacobs

Ralph Lauren bag

THE SCENE

- ★ Scarlett Johansson teamed up with Imitation of Christ designer Tara Subkoff for a jewelry line called S. J. & Tito Jewelry. The line premiered at Subkoff's show.

- ★ There was buzz at the tents that Spring 2007 would be the last at Bryant Park. The Bryant Park Corporation had been disgruntled by the dates of New York Fashion Week ever since the shows were moved from November to September. The corporation didn't like that the park had to be closed for Labor Day for the construction of the tents. Lincoln Center was mentioned as a possibility, but the consensus among the fashion community was to stay in Bryant Park.

- ★ The Delta lounge literally served the fashion community. Color images of Anna Wintour, Vera Wang, Diane von Furstenberg, Richard Tyler, Oscar de la Renta, and Anna Sui were imprinted on cookies given out by the airline.

- ★ Phillip Lim's runway debut had a rocky start, as the crowd had to wait in the dark before they could be seated.

- ★ The MisShapes made their presence known this season. The trio of DJs, Greg Krelenstein, Leigh Lezark, and Geordon Nicol, were hired by both Gwen Stefani and Tory Burch for their shows.

- ★ The previous season, Cathy Horyn of *The New York Times* gave the Carolina Herrera show a bad review. This season the paper was not invited back. Herrera reportedly felt that Horyn's review was something of a personal attack targeting her and her staff. *The New York Times* strongly disagreed.

- ★ Celebrities are able to bypass the crowds and gain immediate entrance to shows. However, Jared Leto chose to forego that privilege and waited in line with the rest of the invitees to get into the Marc Jacobs show.

- ★ James Brown entertained the crowd gathered at Gotham Hall for the Diesel after party.

- ★ Special appearances: Paris and Nicky Hilton, Tinsley Mortimer, Mýa, Johnny Weir, Mena Suvari, Kelis, and Amanda Lepore at Heatherette

Lil Kim and Marc Jacobs

Johnny Weir

ASHLEIGH VERRIER

Designer Ashleigh Verrier graduated Parsons School of Design in 2004 along with designers Chris Benz and Raul Melgoza. Verrier also went to school with Jack McCullough and Lazaro Hernandez of Proenza Schouler (they were seniors when she was a freshman). They brought her on as intern. Upon graduation, the talented Verrier's thesis collection was bought by Saks Fifth Avenue.

EILA MELL: What was your first time showing at New York Fashion Week like?

ASHLEIGH VERRIER: I showed for the first time in Spring 2007 in the UPS Hub. It was a tent they created specifically for emerging talent to show. I was part of a group of ten designers. It was an exciting time. You have this window of fifteen minutes which, in the grand scheme of life, is obviously not a large portion, but it's such a pinnacle moment. When you're doing it for the first time, it's exhilarating.

EM: What does it mean for a designer to show at New York Fashion Week?

AV: Having the opportunity to show as part of Fashion Week gives you leverage as a designer. You're taken a bit more seriously.

EM: What are the weeks leading up to a show like?

AV: It's a combination of extreme focus and extreme chaos. Because I'm a small company, I try to be as organized as I can be in terms of getting the collection finished. But there are always last-minute things, with fittings and maybe deciding to make one last piece. Then there's the PR angle; making sure you're getting the right exposure. The right guest list, retailers, editors, celebrities, socialites, etc. There's definitely a political agenda when it comes to seating arrangements.

EM: What was it like showing at Lincoln Center for the first time for the Spring/Summer 2010 season?

AV: I showed outside, and it worked out really well. It was a beautiful night and we had this garden party, *Gatsby*-like soiree. I love Lincoln Center. I was so pleased with my experience showing there. I think Lincoln Center is synonymous with culture and the arts. It was so amazing to say I was having a fashion show there. I know a lot of people were skeptical; there's always a backlash when there's change, but it was very seamless. Everybody was extremely accommodating and I was thrilled.

PROJECT RUNWAY

IN THE REALITY SERIES *Project Runway*, which debuted in 2004, fashion designers compete for $100,000 to start their own label. The designers are given different challenges on a weekly basis and at the end of each episode one designer is eliminated by host Heidi Klum and her fellow judges, Michael Kors and Nina Garcia. The show finalists get to create a collection which is shown at New York Fashion Week. The Spring 2007 season was *Project Runway*'s third at the tents. By this time the series was a major hit with audiences. The runway show by the finalists was one of the hottest tickets during Fashion Week.

Season three Project Runway winner Jeffrey Sebelia

Heidi Klum

Nina Garcia

CONSTANCE WHITE

Constance White started her career as a reporter for *Women's Wear Daily*. She went on to work at the magazines *Elle* and *Talk*. White has also been a fashion correspondent for *The New York Times*, *British Vogue*, and editor-in-chief of *Essence*. White has made many on-air appearances on shows such as *The Oprah Winfrey Show* and *Project Runway*. White is the style director for eBay, and the author of the book *StyleNoir*.

EILA MELL: What's a typical Fashion Week like for you?

CONSTANCE WHITE: In a word: hectic. It's always exciting to see and to hope to see a great collection. Days are long. During Fashion Week my day usually starts at around 7 AM and ends at 1 AM.

EM: What was the first show you ever attended in New York?

CW: My first show in New York was probably in the early 1990s, when I was a cub reporter at *Women's Wear Daily*. I think it was an Arnold Scaasi fur show. Try topping that.

EM: How does Fashion Week in New York differ from Fashion Week in Europe?

CW: It used to be that the European shows were a lot more cosmopolitan, more United Nations than New York. The tents helped change that. Yet European shows remain more of a mix of people—editors, buyers, stylists, photographers, and so on—from dozens of countries and designers from around the world. New York is more homogenous.

The other major difference is that American shows are pure in their goal of focusing on the clothes and the commercial viability of clothes. European shows do this too, but there is a huge representation of creativity, of theatricality, and of design peculiarities.

EM: What's your take on the skinny model issue?

CW: It's the reality vs. art debate. It reflects larger society. We have this fantasy ideal that has nothing to do with most women and it goes hand in hand with the youth issue. It's difficult and it's disappointing and it's self perpetuating. I don't know how we can stop it but we should try. What's a sixteen-year-old, 5'10", hundred-pound girl got to do with it?

EM: Is it important to have celebrities at fashion shows?

CW: Basically, the fashion industry doesn't need celebrities to function. However, when celebrities wear a designer's clothes it helps sell them, so it's not going to stop anytime soon. Having a celebrity don one of their creations is a validation for some designers.

EM: What do you think of shows being streamed live on the web?

CW: Love it. The Internet continues to push us into new ways to engage the consumer.

EM: Fashion has really emerged into the mainstream over the past few years. Do you think eBay has played a role in that?

CW: eBay has been integral to the mainstreaming of fashion. The auction site made fashion purchases possible for an increasingly sophisticated fashion consumer. As *Sex and the City* made Manolo Blahniks a household name, eBay made Manolos accessible across the country.

EM: How has New York Fashion Week evolved over the years?

CW: New York Fashion Week has become incredibly well organized, centralized, and big! There are more than 300 shows an editor can see in any given show week. Celebrities are now ubiquitous. For better or worse it's become a showcase for non-fashion business as well as stars looking to promote or burnish their images.

EM: Can you tell me some of your favorite memories of New York Fashion Week?

CW: Some of my best New York Fashion Week memories have to include breakthrough shows and fun parties. Interestingly, quite a few of them seem to involve Marc Jacobs—the Marc Jacobs grunge collection; Marc Jacobs taking his bow and onstage beseeching Anna Wintour, sitting a few seats down from me, 'Was it okay?' at the Proenza Schouler show, watching New York's first Internet-to-runway show; watching the first consumer runway show which was staged by Ann Taylor; seeing a perfect collection at Michael Kors; seeing early shows from Phillip Lim, Alexander Wang, and Jason Wu; and a very late Heatherette show.

EM: What would people be surprised to know about Fashion Week?

CW: People who are not in the industry would be shocked to know how demanding the week is and that it's not actually a week as in seven days. It's really closer to nine days.

FRESH FACES

AGYNESS DEYN

FROM: LANCASHIRE, ENGLAND
HEIGHT: 5'8" | HAIR: BLONDE | EYES: BLUE

FRESH FACES

LARA STONE

FROM: GELDROP, NETHERLANDS
HEIGHT: 5'9½" | HAIR: BLONDE
EYES: BROWN

ERIN HEATHERTON

FROM: SKOKIE, ILLINOIS | HEIGHT: 5'11"
HAIR: BLONDE | EYES: GREEN

NEW
ON THE
SCENE

ALEXANDER WANG

Native Californian Alexander Wang launched his first full collection for Spring 2007.

CHRIS BENZ

Chris Benz graduated from Parsons School of Design in 2004, winning the prestigious CFDA Emerging Designer Award.

Marc Jacobs

FALL/WINTER
2007
A GRAY SEASON
PRESENTED FEBRUARY 2–9, 2007

TRENDS: GRAY

EVERYTHING WAS GRAY, from cashmere to felted wools to plain felt. In costume design the use of gray means morally ambiguous. In fashion it means chic.

Michael Kors

Doo.Ri

COLOR POP

A HIT OF intense color with a neutral, a color pop is meant to be a bit of a shock and its use was in full-force for Fall 2007.

PANTS

FALL 2007'S PANTS
were fuller, with higher rises
and waistlines.

Alexander Wang

OTHER HIGHLIGHTS

Michael Kors vest

Preppy at Tommy Hilfiger

THE SCENE

★ Skinny was on people's minds this week. The Council of Fashion Designers of America held a panel discussion on eating disorders. The meeting came one month after the death of model Luisel Ramos, who put herself on a diet of lettuce and diet soda for three months.

Natalia Vodianova addressed the panel. She told of how she was at a high point in her career when, at 5'9", she weighed 106 pounds. But she was anxious and depressed, and her hair was thinning. After seeking help, she "ballooned" up to 112 pounds. She received complaints that she used to be skinnier. Since Vodianova was in demand she was able to stand her ground and keep working. She worried that other models not in her position might be in danger. In response, the CFDA set up guidelines for the industry to follow, although they were only suggestions and not mandatory.

★ Isabel Toledo made her debut as designer for Anne Klein.

★ Diane von Furstenberg showed her first collection as the new president of the CFDA.

★ Heatherette's show was an homage to *The Wizard of Oz*. Lydia Hearst was cast as Dorothy (carrying a real live Toto), while Amanda Lepore was a fabulous Glinda the Good Witch. Included in the collection was clothing that featured images from the film. Designers Richie Rich and Traver Rains took their bow wearing T-shirts that read "There's No Place Like Home" and "We're Not in Kansas Anymore."

★ Douglas Hannant's show at Gotham Hall marked his tenth anniversary in fashion.

★ Nicole Miller celebrated twenty-five years in the fashion industry this season. Fellow designers Carmen Marc Valavo, Dennis Basso, and Joseph Abboud came to her show to celebrate.

★ The Hunter College Gymnasium hosted their first fashion show. Japanese designer Yohji Yamamoto (in collaboration with Adidas) had his Y-3 show at the college.

★ Charlotte Ronson held her show at the dinner theater the Box. As guests settled into the tightly crowded space, someone accidentally pushed one of the waitresses into a candle. Her hair caught on fire, but she quickly put it out and was safe.

★ The *Today* show's Natalie Morales was one of the celebrities modeling in the Heart Truth show. When Morales got to the end of the runway she did a twirl and her Tracy Reese dress flew up, inadvertently flashing the audience, which included First Lady Laura Bush. Morales, a good sport, was later teased about it by co-host Al Roker on *Today*.

★ Milanese designer Alberta Ferretti brought her Philosophy show to New York for the first time.

★ Zooey Deschanel opened Erin Fetherston's show by singing "Dream a Little Dream."

★ A crowd gathered outside Cipriani, where Rock & Republic's show was held. Guests showed up about an hour before show time, but security wouldn't let anyone in until five minutes before the start. The line of people (which extended beyond the length of a city block) had to brave the February cold until they could be admitted.

★ Special Appearances: Spring Awakening's John Gallagher and Jonathan Groff walking for Jill Stuart.

COCO ROCHA

In a few short years, Coco Rocha went from fashion newcomer to one of the top models in the world. She has worked with photographers such as Patrick Demarchelier, Steven Meisel, Steven Klein, Arthur Elgort, and Annie Leibovitz. Rocha's talent is not limited to modeling. She is an accomplished Irish dancer, as she demonstrated at Jean Paul Gaultier's Fall/Winter 2007 show. *Vogue* labeled it the Coco Moment.

EILA MELL: How did you get your start as a model?

COCO ROCHA: I was first spotted by an agent in Vancouver at an Irish Dance competition. At first when he approached me about being a model I thought he was joking; I was the least fashion savvy of my friends. He persisted and asked another couple times and finally my mother let me give it a try.

EM: What was the first show you walked in at New York Fashion Week?

CR: I think my first season was Fall/Winter 2005. I remember my first big show in the tents was AsFour and I was thinking that this "runway walking" would be easy—just put one foot in front of the other and walk in a straight line. I was the second one out and had only gone a few steps before I started feeling dizzy. I immediately started over thinking exactly how one does put one foot down in front of the other. In what felt like an eternity, but which lasted only moments, I pulled it together and got the job done.

EM: You've also covered Fashion Week as a reporter. What is it like being on the other side of the runway?

CR: It was very different from my usual experience backstage, but I feel like I had a nice little advantage over other reporters. For one, I knew very well how busy those people were so I like to think I was a more considerate reporter than some are used to. It was also very easy for me to chat with my friends, the models. Generally models are quite shy about speaking to reporters, so being "one of them" gave me an edge.

EM: You've spoken out about models' weight issues. Not long after it began getting a lot of media attention, Marc Jacobs and Prada showed more womanly silhouettes. Do you think there's been an improvement?

CR: It certainly seems that way. Not only in that aspect, but I also see much more diversity as far as the age range of the models and their ethnic background. It's good news because it means we all have a place in fashion, not just one particular "type." Will it stay this way? No, not forever, but that's fashion. It's always changing.

EM: What's a typical Fashion Week (or month, with all the cities) like for you?

CR: It's not as bad as it used to be. When I was starting out, I would do more than sixty shows a season or some ridiculous number like that! These days I take Fashion Week at a much gentler pace. Generally I'll do just one or two shows a day, so it's not bad at all. New York Fashion Week is very easy since I'm in my hometown and it becomes a little reunion of all my old friends. London is next, and everyone is still in high spirits. By the time we get to Milan we are all a little more irritable and the city is a nightmare to get around. Once we are in Paris we're all delirious and so turned around, but there are fun parties in Paris, and of course amazing shows. By the time the fashion *month* is over we are all ready for a vacation.

EM: What would people be surprised to know about New York Fashion Week?

CR: That in general we models don't get paid. Everyone thinks we make a ton of money over Fashion Week, but in reality most of us make nothing at all. Occasionally we will get clothes out of the deal, but mostly we do it as favors to the designers and also to get our image out there.

FRESH FACES

DAUL KIM

FROM: SEOUL, SOUTH KOREA | HEIGHT:
5'10" | HAIR: BROWN | EYES: BROWN

KASIA STRUSS

FROM: CIECHANÓW, POLAND | HEIGHT:
5' 10½" | HAIR: BROWN | EYES: BROWN

DOUGLAS HANNANT

Douglas Hannant studied design at FIT. He got his start in fashion working as an assistant window dresser under Simon Doonan at Barneys. In 1996 he started his collection. Hannant is known for his impeccable tailoring and luxurious fabrics.

EILA MELL: What was your first time showing at New York Fashion Week like?

DOUGLAS HANNANT: I was very nervous and not yet jaded. My first show prior was at Geoffrey Beene's showroom. He invited me to show there.

EM: Do you have a favorite collection?

DH: Always the last one that I have done.

EM: Are there any other designers whose shows you regularly attend?

DH: I hate to go to fashion shows.

EM: What do you look for in models?

DH: Regal, a sense of privilege and tiny features. They should carry height in their legs, not torso, and only 5'9" to 5'11". I believe they are like athletes and must be in runway shape.

EM: How long after showing a collection do you get to work on the next one?

DH: The next day.

Kimora Lee

Lydia Hearst

SNAPPED!

Natalie Morales

Zooey Deschanel and Erin Fetherston

Heatherette

SPRING/SUMMER
2008
A SEXY SEASON
PRESENTED SEPTEMBER 5–12, 2007

TRENDS:
ASYMMETRY

THERE WAS A Gianni Versace feel to the asymmetry shown for Spring/Summer 2008. Clothes were sexy; skin exposed.

Erin Fetherston

Heatherette

LINGERIE

LINGERIE WAS ALWAYS right for a spring collection. Designers harkened back to Madonna, with underwear as outerwear. This time around though, it was done in a soft way. There were no Jean Paul Gaultier cone bras to be seen.

SAFARI

THE SAFARI TREND has always come and gone in fashion. This season it was modernized with the use of unusual fabrics and colors.

Rag & Bone

Diane von Furstenberg

Donna Karan Collection

Erin Fetherston's headgear

OTHER HIGHLIGHTS

Erin Fetherston's snowy eyes

Charlotte Ronson's glasses

TRACY REESE

Tracy Reese graduated Parsons School of Design in 1984 and started her own company in 1987. She has also designed for the labels Perry Ellis and Maga-schoni. In 2007 Reese was inducted as a board member of the CFDA.

EILA MELL: What was your breakthrough as a designer?

TRACY REESE: Coming to New York to study at Parsons really was the jumping off part to make my dream of becoming a clothing designer a reality. I learned the foundations of making it in fashion working with Martine Sitbon at Arlequin Paris and as women's design director at Perry Ellis Portfolio before going out on my own. I can't name just a single moment, but opening my own store—and dressing Michelle Obama for the cover of *People*—certainly stand out!

EM: Do you have a signature piece?

TR: Dresses are my signature; they are easy, comfortable, and provide a total look without too much effort. I believe that a fabulous dress that can be worn from day to evening is a must. I love using beautiful color combinations and luxurious fabrics and embellishments that enhance and celebrate all women.

EM: How does clothing go from the runway to retail?

TR: It's a long journey and much more complex than most people realize. Each item of clothing goes through multiple fittings on a size eight model until the fit is perfected for mass production. We also continue to work on the technical aspects of each garment, including fabrication, trim, and overall workmanship. Our goal is to ship the highest quality garments possible for the price points we are offering. It can be challenging.

EM: How do you combine being a creative person with also being a business person?

TR: I think that in order to run a successful design house, you must be educated on both sides of the industry. At Parsons we were not taught the business side of fashion. I've had to learn a lot through trial and error. Without a balance of both, it is hard to be successful. I thought I knew everything, but I learned quickly that I really didn't, and knew I had to learn more about business.

EM: Who are your influences?

TR: Strong women, like my mother and grandmother, have always influenced me. They believed in me, supported me, and pushed me to pursue my dreams. From my early days of designing, and still today, I love to create pieces that are vibrant and elegant, paying close attention to detail. I want women to feel great in what they wear, and as a woman designer, I am constantly inspired to come up with clothing that can enhance a woman's confidence.

EM: What was your style growing up?

TR: My personal style has always been feminine with vintage and bohemian influence. My mother had a rule that I had to wear a dress to school at least three days out of five and I think that still influences me now!

EM: What impact does Fashion Week have on your business?

TR: Fashion Week is the Super Bowl of the fashion industry—editors, buyers, and fans come to preview what is new for the upcoming season. Having a runway show allows us, our buyers, and critics the opportunity to see the collection as a whole, in motion, with our choice of accessories, hair, makeup, etc. The dream comes to life! It reminds us why we are doing this, because the day-to-day work is much more diffused and we don't often get to see the whole picture.

THE SCENE

* Behnaz Sarafpour felt so ill on her way to her show that her husband called an ambulance. The designer was taken to Beth Israel Medical Center, where she learned she had a kidney stone. She was sent home that evening, but had to miss her show. She was able to watch it on style.com.

* Marc Jacobs started his show off with his curtain call. The models then came out for the finale, and worked their way backwards to the first look.

* Ralph Lauren marked his fortieth anniversary in fashion with a beautiful show and black-tie after party at the Central Park Conservatory. Lauren closed his show with the song "The Best is Yet to Come" and was greeted with a standing ovation from the appreciative crowd. The show's backdrop then opened up to reveal a garden set up with tables to accommodate his four hundred guests.

* Helmut Lang was re-launched this season. Designers Michael and Nicole Colovos were brought on to create the looks in the spirit of Lang's original designs.

* Once again Italian designer Alberta Ferretti showed her Philosophy line in New York. In fact, Ferretti announced that the city would become the permanent home for the label's shows.

* The British label Preen made its New York debut.

* Anna Sui's gift bag included a T-shirt which read "Forever Wanted: Don Cassidy & The Sundance Jin, Reward $21,000" and "Thou shalt not steal; Exodus 20:15." The reference was to the retail chain Forever 21's owners Don and Jin Chang, who Sui filed a suit against for copyright infringement.

* Betsey Johnson celebrated the prom at her Spring 2008 show. Her invitation had a picture of Johnson at her own high school prom on it. Guests were seated at tables and given mini Moët & Chandon bottles to accentuate the theme. The show itself went decade by decade with 1950s-inspired fashions through to the present day.

* The two-hour wait for the start of the Marc Jacobs show had many guests upset. Rumors spread that while his audience was kept waiting Jacobs was at the bar of the Mercer Hotel. Robert Duffy (Marc Jacobs International president) vehemently denied this, saying that he was with Jacobs at the Armory, where the show was held. Jacobs publicly apologized for the delay, but explained that the early dates of Fashion Week made it very difficult to accomplish all that was necessary to get done for the three shows he presented this season—Marc Jacobs, Marc by Marc Jacobs, and men's Marc by Marc Jacobs.

* Led by former model and model agent Bethann Hardison, the Bryant Park Hotel hosted a discussion called the Lack of the Black Image in Fashion Today. The standing-room crowd discussed the issue of discrimination in the fashion business. The issue was so important to Naomi Campbell that she flew in from London to be there. Hardison said that the current time was the worst the industry had seen. The purpose of the discussion was to bring awareness to this issue.

* Special appearances: Lil' Mama, Kim Kardashian, Amanda Lepore, and Jenna Jameson at Heatherette

Janet Jackson

Ralph and Ricky Lauren

Nicole and Michael Colovos

Kim Kardashian at Heatherette

Betsey Johnson

BETHANN HARDISON

Designer Willi Smith discovered Bethann Hardison in an elevator. She became his fit model, and eventually went on to become a full-time model. Hardison appeared in top magazines such as *Vogue* and *Harper's Bazaar*. She later became a model agent and later opened her own agency, Bethann Management. In the late 1980s, she cofounded the Black Girls Coalition with her friend, supermodel Iman. The Coalition was initially organized to celebrate black models working in the fashion industry, but eventually worked to address the problem of a lack of diversity. Although retired by 2010, Hardison is still active. In 2008 she was a contributing editor to *Vogue Italia*'s famous all-black issue.

EILA MELL: You've spoken out about the lack of diversity on the runway. Can you tell me about that?

BETHANN HARDISON: When I would have lunch with certain editors they would tell me there are no blacks on the runway anymore. This was in 1997, 1998. By 2004, I got a call from Naomi Campbell. She said, "You really have to do something. It's terrible. There're no black girls on the runway at all." I got another phone call from André Leon Talley and he said the same thing. After two years of hearing this I decided to hold a town hall meeting and press conference. That started to make things shift.

EM: Who was there?

BH: It was everyone from fashion editors to writers, models, agents, casting directors, designers, press, and photographers. Naomi flew in from London. That morning I made ten points about things that were going on in the industry that made me uncomfortable. That took place on September 14, 2007. Then on October 14 we had a huge meeting of about three hundred people at the New York Public Library. It was packed. We had an adjacent room for people to view it on a monitor. We held a panel discussion with a casting director, a model agent, a designer, and a stylist. I moderated. We made the front page of *The New York Times* Style Section. By the next

season, no one ever said no blacks, no ethnics anymore.

EM: Do you think the problem was limited to black models or other minorities as well?

BH: At one point mine was the only agency in New York that had an Asian girl. There are Asian designers that don't even use Asian models. The runways are more diverse than they were a few years ago, but it needs to get better.

EM: Are there models that transcend race?

BH: Naomi Campbell is a black model they can't deny. She has longevity, she's iconic. But will she make as much money as her white counterparts? Oftentimes not. Did she have to work very hard to make sure she got paid the right money in her time coming up as a model? She did. Can she get a cover as easy as a white girl? No, she can't because she's still of color. Yes, everyone wants to know about her; but even though she is Naomi Campbell, she still may not get a beauty campaign over a white girl.

EM: She's done such wonderful charitable work with her Fashion for Relief shows. What was it like for you to work on those shows with her?

BH: They were really extraordinary shows. It was amazing how she pulled the first one off. She had an idea to raise consciousness and money for the victims of Hurricane Katrina. She called right after it happened and wanted to pull it off in two weeks. I thought it was completely impossible, but she gathered the people. IMG gave her the tent. They were very good to donate it. She just called people to participate. Her goal was always to raise $1 million. She got it done. We did the same thing for Haiti. Naomi's someone who drives things, and she will make it happen.

SNAPPED!

Victoria Beckham

Sarah Jessica Parker, Matthew Broderick, and Robert De Niro

Ralph Lauren

FALL/WINTER
2008
ANYTHING GOES
PRESENTED FEBRUARY 1–8, 2008

TRENDS:
ECCENTRIC

EVERYTHING BUT THE kitchen sink fashion was in for Fall 2008. This was not a moment for wallflowers—blending in was not an option.

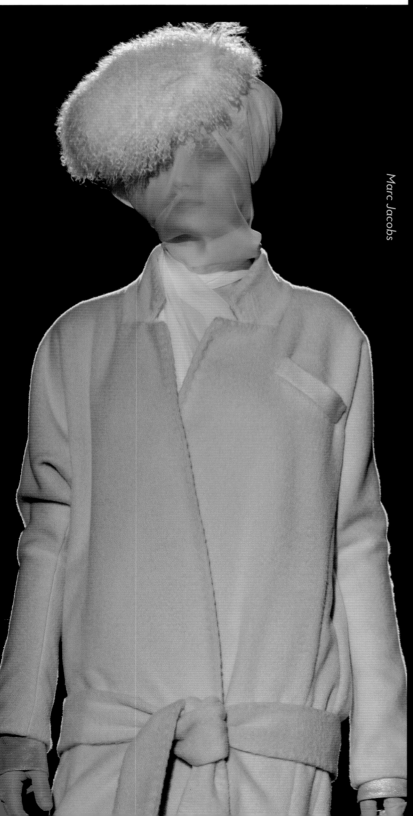

Marc Jacobs

Rodarte

TOUGH CHIC

FALL/WINTER 2008 saw an aggressive, masculine take on tough chic.

Diane von Furstenberg

Alexander Wang

RETRO REWIND

NO SINGLE DECADE dominated as designers presented styles from several different eras.

GEORGINA CHAPMAN

Georgina Chapman grew up in London, England. While in art school she met Keren Craig. The two joined forces, and in 2004 launched their line, Marchesa, named after the eccentric Italian aristocrat Marchesa Luisa Casati. The label took off immediately and has since become a fixture on the red carpet. Celebrities such as Sarah Jessica Parker, Blake Lively, Jennifer Lopez, Demi Moore, Rihanna, Sandra Bullock, and Renee Zellweger have all worn Marchesa.

EILA MELL: Did you always want to be a designer?

GEORGINA CHAPMAN: I've always wanted to be a designer, since a very young age, and have loved fashion for as long as I can remember. I attended art college to pursue this passion, where I originally started as a costume designer and then transitioned into fashion.

EM: Is there a favorite fabric you love to work with?

GC: We work with so many different types of fabrics and are always looking to source new and original textiles, but some of the signature Marchesa fabrics include various forms of satin, lace, tulle, and organza.

EM: What was it like showing at New York Fashion Week for the first time?

GC: It was quite exhilarating! I was thrilled and nervous at the same time. Overall, it was a very proud moment. Showing at New York Fashion Week is a huge accomplishment for any designer.

EM: What's the most enjoyable part about designing a collection?

GC: I love everything about designing. It's not only a great outlet to channel my inspiration and creativity, but I enjoy challenging myself to continually evolve my collections. I love everything from the research phase to draping and experimenting with different silhouettes or fabric treatments. The process is always exciting.

THE SCENE

★ Model Erin Wasson served as the stylist for Alexander Wang's show.

★ Liza Minnelli showed up to celebrate the re-launch of Halston at the Gagosian Gallery. Minnelli and Roy Halston Frowick were dear friends. Minnelli had kind words for the label's new designer, Marco Zanini, saying that he honored the memory of her late friend.

★ Seventeen years after the iconic designer's death, Halston's fashion house was taken over by Harvey Weinstein, with Jimmy Choo, designer Tamara Mellon, and stylist Rachel Zoe on his team.

★ Halston and net-a-porter.com made a groundbreaking deal that the website would sell two of the show's looks the day after their debut on the runway.

★ Vera Wang introduced her lower-priced line, Lavender Label, at the townhouse restaurant Bobo on West 10th Street.

★ Yigal Azrouël's show included a film by Chiara Clemente as the backdrop. Azrouël met Clemente for the first time about two weeks before the show, and decided then and there to make the film with Chiara.

★ Rather than a traditional runway show, Marc Bouwer showed his new line on his website, marcbouwer.com.

★ New to New York this season was Jonathan Saunders. Saunders moved his show from London, and chose the Tunnel as the venue for his stateside debut.

★ Models Irina Lazareanu, Iekeliene Stange, and Angelika Kocheva all wore Global Action for Children T-shirts backstage during Fashion Week. The hope was to raise awareness of the organization, which mobilizes government support and community action on behalf of children in need.

Then First Lady Laura Bush at The Heart Truth Show

MARIA PINTO

Designer Maria Pinto is a graduate of Chicago's School of the Art Institute, Parsons School of Design, and the Fashion Institute of Technology (FIT). Soon after graduation, Pinto went to work for legendary designer Geoffrey Beene. She launched her label, Maria Pinto, in 1991 with a collection of accessories at Bergdorf Goodman. First Lady Michelle Obama famously wore Pinto's designs on two momentous occasions: when Barack Obama won the Democratic presidential nomination, and when she made a speech at the Democratic National Convention.

EILA MELL: How do you approach design?

MARIA PINTO: The most important aspect of my design is honoring a woman's body. Age doesn't matter, body type doesn't matter. I just try to design very beautiful things that are comfortable and functional.

EM: Who has been your biggest creative influence?

MP: It's usually artists, although my last collection was inspired by tango. That was a departure and it was very exciting.

EM: How does that translate to your design?

MP: The inspiration is a subliminal tool to move forward from the previous season. It can be the tension, the emotion, and it influences the color palette.

EM: Are wearable clothes your goal?

MP: There's a part of me that loves the aspect of fantasy, allowing a woman to escape, but I also want to be aware of what we need as women. I'm a little too practical to not address that.

EM: Are there any colors you tend to repeat?

MP: Not really. I just like to juxtapose different colors together, and that's what I encourage my clients to do—and to always add color to your wardrobe every season because I think it uplifts us.

EM: How do you feel when you see a woman on the street in your clothes?

MP: I love it! I've even approached them.

EM: What was it like to dress Michelle Obama?

MP: It was wonderful. I love having fabulous women like Michelle Obama, Oprah Winfrey, and Marcia Gay Harden wear my clothes.

FRESH FACES

ANNA GUSHINA

FROM: RUSSIA | HEIGHT: 5' 9" | HAIR: BROWN | EYES: BLUE

HELOISE GUERIN

FROM: FRANCE | HEIGHT: 5'11"
HAIR: BLONDE | EYES: BLUE

MALIN ONES

FROM: LANGHUS, NORWAY | HEIGHT:
5' 11" | HAIR: BLONDE | EYES: BLUE

RAD HOURANI

Former stylist and self-taught designer Rad Hourani launched his label in 2007. In just a few short years, Hourani established himself as a designer of unisex clothing. Anna Dello Russo, Jessica Alba, and Lady Gaga have been photographed in his designs.

EILA MELL: Do you design with yourself in mind?

RAD HOURANI: Absolutely. It's what I feel like wearing.

EM: And that's both men's and women's?

RH: I don't consider myself a man or a woman; I think I'm just a human on the planet. It's a bit limiting to say a man or a woman or an age. I can be feminine; I can be masculine.

EM: Jessica Alba was photographed in your clothes. Do you think she exemplifies your style?

RH: Yes. Anybody can wear the clothes, you just have to understand them, feel them. She's a curvy, sexy woman, a femme fatale. She can fit the clothes and make it modern. Anybody can do that. The clothes are for everyone. You don't have to be androgynous; you don't have to be curvy. One of my best clients is sixty-five years old. She's super curvy and she feels good in the clothes. She's not an androgynous woman. A very masculine man can also wear the clothes.

EM: Do you ever feel pressured to design a dress for the red carpet?

RH: There are so many people that do that, they don't need me.

Ali Hewson and Bono

Leigh Lezark

Keren Craig, Anne Hathaway, and Georgina Chapman

SNAPPED!

Max Azria

Grace Coddington, Anna Wintour, and Sally Singer

Rachel Roy

SPRING/SUMMER

2009

RECESSION FASHION

PRESENTED SEPTEMBER 5-12, 2008

TRENDS:
BACK TO BASICS

WITH AMERICA IN a recession, designers went back to basics to answer the customer's needs.

Cushnie et Ochs

DKNY

Doo.Ri

EXOTICISM

IN A TOUGH economic time customers could look to designers to fulfill the fantasy of travel and exotic locations.

Ralph Lauren

Donna Karan Collection

GODDESS

MODELS SHOWED A nod to Madame Grès, typified by draping in soft fabrics like jersey and silk. The so-called "easy" look takes a highly skilled designer to achieve.

Lauren Hutton modeling in the Be EcoChic Show

Marc Jacobs hat

Narciso Rodriguez's dress

OTHER HIGHLIGHTS

The Wizard of Oz Ruby Slipper Collection, celebrating the film's seventieth anniversary

★ The backdrop of Nanette Lepore's show read "Save the Garment Center." Lepore took her stand even further by having "Save the Garment Center" buttons, pencils, and T-shirts for her staff.

★ Alan Cumming and Heather Graham emceed the G-Star Raw show. It opened with Cumming and Graham speaking about the United Nations Millennium Campaign to end poverty.

★ For Sophie Theallet's first ever runway show she decided to use a cast of only black models. Theallet felt that the colors she used would look best on dark skin.

★ Designer Scott Sternberg, of the Band of Outsiders label, eschewed a traditional runway show this season. He instead directed actors Kirsten Dunst and Max Minghella and musician Charles Hamilton wearing his clothes in a video which played as guests looked through racks of his designs.

★ Olympic gymnast Alicia Sacramone attended the BCBG Max Azria show with a special trinket on hand—her silver medal.

★ Members of PETA interrupted the DKNY show with signs reading "Donna: Dump Fur." The protest also took place outside, with demonstrators dressed as animals covered in blood.

★ Miss NYC Plus, a pageant for plus size women, held a demonstration outside of Tracy Reese's show. They wore shirts which read: "There's nothing negative about being a plus."

★ Guests at L'Wren Scott's show got an extra treat. Scott's boyfriend, Mick Jagger, wrote two songs specifically for the show called "You Run Run Run Me Ragged" and "Fly, Oh My Sweet Angel."

★ *Project Runway* winner Christian Siriano showed his Spring 2009 collection with some friends in the audience. The show's stars, Heidi Klum, Tim Gunn, and Nina Garcia were on hand to cheer him on.

Lady Bunny

Vanessa Williams

Robert Tagliapietra
and Jeffrey Costello

NEW ON THE SCENE

FRESH FACE

ALTUZARRA

Paris-born Joseph Altuzarra worked at Givenchy, where he met Coline Choay, the label's public relations manager. She left the company to help Altuzarra launch his own label, which he showed for the first time for the Spring 2009 season.

IMOGEN MORRIS CLARKE

FROM: LONDON, ENGLAND | HEIGHT: 5'10"
HAIR: BROWN | EYES: HAZEL

KATIE FOGARTY

Katie Fogarty began modeling in 2008, signing with Next Management in New York. That same year she would be walking for Ohne Titel, Marc by Marc Jacobs, and Philosophy di Alberta Ferretti. Balancing a life as a full-time student and full-time model, Katie became a muse for Balenciaga and BCBG Max Azria.

EILA MELL: How did you get into modeling?

KATIE FOGARTY: When I was thirteen I was scouted by Jeff and Mary Clarke in a mall in St. Louis. Two years later I went to New York with Next modeling agency.

EM: Is there a difference between working with veteran designers and new designers?

KF: When working with a veteran designer such as Miuccia Prada or Oscar de la Renta, a wave of respect floats from everyone in the room. They know what they want, and know how to take risks without jeopardizing sales. Newer designers know no boundaries and are not tied to any specific aesthetic. They are still establishing "their woman" and can change their design concepts easily.

EM: What is the relationship between model and designer like?

KF: For me, it's all about respect for a designer. To do my job I must be a blank canvas, quiet, but energetic. I try to find out what type of woman the designer wants to portray and play that role.

EM: How does Fashion Week in New York compare to those in other cities?

KF: New York Fashion Week is by far the best in my opinion. Not only is it the first, but it has the added bonus of being in America. People are their most fresh, friendly, and exciting during New York Fashion Week. Also, New York has the best catering.

EM: What is it like backstage during a show?

KF: Backstage can be two scenes—waiting around forever chatting with the other models, or coming in five minutes before the show starts straight to hair and makeup double duty.

EM: I've heard that it's pretty common for models to be late to a show. Is that stressful?

KF: In our defense, it's not our fault! We're not out shopping or watching a movie! Usually it's because another fitting/casting/show ran late. It has happened to me many times. I hate being late. When I can, I always arrive around call time. Why add more stress to my day?

EM: What would people be surprised to know about models?

KF: Most of us are students and normal teenagers that like to play sports and talk about films and books. The majority of models I meet are super friendly!

EM: What's your take on the skinny model issue?

KF: Well, most of the super slim girls are just that: slim girls. They are sixteen years old eating whatever they want when they want. The rest of the girls stay healthy through normal exercise and diet. The reason why we became models is we have slim and lanky bodies. I think it is really important for people to know that most models are skinny because we are energetic, active human beings who would care about our health and eating habits even if we weren't models.

EM: What would people be surprised to know about New York Fashion Week?

KF: People would be surprised to know that we do not find out our schedules for the next day until sometimes 3 AM!

Anna Sui

FALL/WINTER
2009

AN EXOTIC SEASON

PRESENTED FEBRUARY 13-20, 2009

TRENDS:
SHOULDERS

EUROPEAN INFLUENCE WAS felt in the use of a strong shoulders, either overextended or pagoda.

Derek Lam

Miss Sixty

Marc Jacobs

RUCHING

THIS COUTURE TECHNIQUE was seen in trousers, jackets, dresses, and blouses.

BIKERS AND ROCKERS

THIS WAS THE fashion version of bikers and rockers. These expensive leathers had a great deal of detail, with studs, belts, buckles, etc.

Nicholas K

Miss Sixty

FALL/WINTER 2009 **319**

Isaac Mizrahi's bag

Makeup at Marc Jacobs

OTHER HIGHLIGHTS

Marchesa's bows

The Barbie show, celebrating the iconic doll's fiftieth anniversary

VERYO
NEEDS
A
KEN!

Proenza Schouler's clutch

THE SCENE

★ Ashley Dupre, best known as New York governor Eliot Spitzer's call girl, made a surprise appearance in the front row of Yigal Azrouël's first show in the tents. Azrouël's publicist, Kelly Cutrone, saw Dupre and immediately knew that she should not be seated there. Cutrone asked Dupre to move back a row. Right before the start of the show, Cutrone checked back to see how things were out front and saw that Dupre was still seated in the front. She made the decision that Dupre could stay put, although she knew the potential for controversy. After the show, Dupre made her way backstage, where photographers took her picture with Azrouël.

　　After the Azrouël show there was a champagne toast at the Mercedes Benz lounge, where the designer toasted Cutrone, praising the hard work she put in to make the show possible. Later on that night though, Cutrone received a call from the designer, who was livid at Dupre's presence at his show. Cutrone and Azrouël cut ties not long after.

★ Many designers scaled back their shows this season as a reaction to the recession. For example, the Marc Jacobs show, which typically had a guest list of two thousand, cut back to about seven hundred invitees, and he had a less elaborate set than in seasons past.

★ Another way designers cut costs was to eliminate after parties.

★ The rumor that New York Fashion Week would move from Bryant Park to Lincoln Center was confirmed by Mayor Michael Bloomberg at a press conference held by IMG Fashion and the CFDA. The shows would remain in the park for another year, and debut uptown in September 2010.

　　The fashion industry had mixed reactions to news of the move to Lincoln Center. While some worried that the new location was too far from the Garment Center, others embraced the chance to have Fashion Week incorporated into the cultural epicenter of New York City.

★ QVC hosted their own live runway show, where viewers had the opportunity to order garments right off the runway. Some of the labels featured were Logo by Lori Goldstein, M by Marc Bouwer, A List by Alvin Valley, and Elisabeth Hasselbeck for Dialogue.

★ Model Coco Rocha turned reporter when she was hired by the E! network to cover the shows.

★ Musician Max de Castro flew in from Brazil to perform at his friend Carlos Miele's runway show.

★ After several of his models had trouble walking in their heels, designer Brian Reyes sent them all out for the finale barefoot.

KELLY CUTRONE

Kelly Cutrone is the founder of the fashion public relations, branding, and marketing firm People's Revolution. Her agency has produced shows for artists like Alexandre Herchcovitch, Rachel Comey, AsFour, Patricia Field, Atil Kutoglu, Marissa Ribisi, Alvin Valley, Nicky Hilton, Paco Rabanne, and Vivienne Westwood. Cutrone is the star of the reality series *Kell on Earth* and the author of *If You Have to Cry Go Outside: And Other Things Your Mother Never Told You.*

EILA MELL: How does People's Revolution work?

KELLY CUTRONE: Our agency is a little different from most public relations companies. They go out and decide this is who they want to represent. They call up the people like Sonia Rykiel. I just would never do that, I don't know why; I just never wanted to pitch anybody. I guess I don't like the idea of somebody saying "no" to me. So our business comes through referral. Once we decide to work with a designer it is our job to produce a fashion show for them.

EM: What goes into that?

KC: We help the designer edit themselves. We become the eyes and ears of the consumer, and then keepers of the gate, and then ultimately the retailers and the editors. We try to steer and veer the client into producing an event that is going to be agreeable to the public. If they're going to do a show at 9:00 AM, we're going to suggest they use some kind of nice popular music like "A Horse with No Name" instead of German death metal. We want to try and find the right venue for them, that will reflect the brand and the collection at hand. We work to get them the best timeslot, the best venue, and the best price. We oversee the models: who is going to be casting the show and what the models are going to look like. We lock down the hair and makeup people so they can set a tone and work with the designer. The stylist comes in to try to add freshness to the collection, add a point of view, and do accessories. We are in charge of inviting all the press and the seating arrangements. We direct the show. We receive and transport the collection. We're in charge of the gift bags and the crews that are going to be invited to do backstage interviews to cover the shows. And we handle everything that happens during the fashion show and follow up afterward, and then post the press, too.

EM: So there's a lot of pressure to deal with.

KC: Everything that happens is your fault. If it's good, then the designer is great. If it's not it's because you suck. It's masochism from the get go. If you are looking for flowers, a "please" or a "thank you," this is probably not the right job.

EM: What's it like directing a show?

KC: It's awesome. It's like being an air-traffic controller. It's like when you're a rock star and you get to be in the stadium, and you're having your show and everything feels really good. It's thirteen minutes of—sometimes terror, but when things are going well it's awesome.

EM: What goes into doing the seating chart?

KC: You decide who is going to sit where. Then you have to email and let everybody know what their seat assignment is.

EM: Have people gotten upset if they think they should have gotten a better seat?

KC: Some people are thankful and happy to be invited to one of these exclusive events. Others become violent, saying there must be a mistake because they're actually a front-row person. People steal other people's seats. I actually started arguing and fighting a lot. Then we do the bounce. That's where I tell someone they are in the wrong seat and I count to three. If they won't get up I have security take them out. That's the most productive, non-violent way. Now people are so scared of me I don't even have to say anything. They jump out of the seats.

EM: What's your opinion of the celebrity presence at the shows?

KC: I think it's great. It's business. Everyone is out for themselves. I don't think that most of the celebrities that go care about fashion. There are a few really diehard fashion girls like Chloë Sevigny and the Olsen girls. They work in the fashion industry. They love it. They spend a fortune on clothes.

Some people go because they are getting paid to go there, and others go because they know that they need to be associated with fashion so brands will look at them as endorsable; so companies like Maybelline, L'Oréal, and Toyota will want them for their campaigns. They are there for themselves and their career and they want free things. It's business for them.

EM: What's your take on the skinny model issue?

KC: Some girls are naturally thin. They just are. I've seen models eat a lot. I think that society is to blame. Our society values, endorses, and glorifies thinness. The fashion industry is just trying to give consumers what they want. There is a lot of pressure on the models, but that is their job. Their job is to be skinny and fit the clothes.

I don't want to see any person try to be something they can barely be and hurt themselves though. If you don't like to walk in high shoes, and you don't like people pulling on your hair and putting makeup on your face and pushing you, saying "Go, go," and you don't like to be skinny or you can't be naturally, then you shouldn't be a model. It's like a hockey player not fitting

his skates. I know that sounds cruel, but that is the reality of the business.

EM: Do you think your Bravo show, *Kell on Earth*, is a good representation of what actually goes on in the fashion industry?

KC: My show was too accurate about what goes on. I don't think that people want to hear about a broken printer for fifteen minutes. That's a very real show. The interns not knowing how to fold, models passing out, tangling up a Swarovski crystal curtain—all genuine.

EM: How has the industry evolved since you started?

KC: Fashion used to be for a very small group of people. Halston was one of the first people to mass market the concept of fashion design for people in America. Now it's everywhere. It's for everybody.

EM: As a mother, do you have any reservations about bringing your daughter around fashion?

KC: No. This is one of the few businesses where women are in charge. You very rarely notice, but if you look in PR and production it's definitely women and gay men. She sees a lot of women in power. She sees the need for collaboration. She sees the music people, the video people, models, shoe designers, jewelry designers, the guy who comes in with the van. She's learned so much.

There is a beautiful side to the industry in terms of lineage. You can't learn it. You have to be part of it. The women are all different ages. When I had my daughter the models would come by when I was breast feeding. They were about sixteen, closer to the baby's age than to mine, but at the same time they are working with prestigious women. There are all these beautiful women, like Odile Gilbert, and you can't believe you're in the same room with them. It's really like a weird, beautiful carnival. You are traveling with these people and you're all looking out for each other. It's very tribal and it's beautiful.

NEW ON THE SCENE

FRESH FACE

RANYA MORDANOVA

FROM: UFA, RUSSIA | HEIGHT: 5'9"
HAIR: BROWN | EYES: BROWN

PRABAL GURUNG

Designer Prabal Gurung described the customer for his debut collection as a thinking-man's sex symbol.

LORENZO MARTONE

Lorenzo Martone grew up in São Paulo, Brazil. He moved to Paris in 2004, where he earned his MBA. In 2009 he and business partner Ryan Brown opened ARC New York, a boutique talent and PR company.

EILA MELL: How does New York Fashion Week compare to European Fashion Weeks?

LORENZO MARTONE: I compare Fashion Weeks to the actual cultures of the countries. It's really beautiful what they do in Europe. Things are handcrafted and it's very rich. But I always feel like there's not enough focus on business. In New York Fashion Week there is a lot of creativity, but there is less of that handiwork. Americans are doers, they're achievers, and they make it happen. America is a much younger place. There's more energy. In Europe, they've been there, done that. Now they're more reserved.

EM: How did the recession affect the industry?

LM: People were doing shows without having anything to show; without a point of view. The recession showed that you could be more creative and you didn't need to put together a $500,000 fashion show. You can show in a different way. If you're not coming with a point of view or a strong design aesthetic then don't waste your time. Ten days of fashion shows is way too many.

EM: What excites you about fashion?

LM: I love when designers use cultural references and when there's a story behind a collection from something in the past. Houses that do just purely design with no references become uninteresting very quickly because they're based on trends. There's no emotional benefit to the clothes.

EM: Your company, ARC New York, represents Alessandra Ambrosio, who is best known as a Victoria's Secret model. She recently started doing more runway shows. Are designers embracing curves again?

LM: Alessandra has a perfect body, and she exemplifies this embrace of real women again. It started Fall 2010 with Prada. They were casting girls who were more in the commercial realm of fashion. It's been a huge success because people can relate more to someone like Alessandra than to a super-skinny model. Nowadays fashion houses have realized that models with curves can wear clothes so well and look healthy. It creates an optimistic sort of vibe. It's like the supermodels. There can be a new generation of supermodels who cannot only wear clothes well, but express their personality and their personal style. The way celebrities invaded fashion, I think fashion models should invade the pop culture world.

EM: If you could only go to one show during New York Fashion Week what would it be?

LM: I always support people I love so of course it would be Marc [Jacobs].

EM: I'm always amazed that he has three lines, and they're all so different.

LM: When I went to school I learned that one of the business models is the pyramid model. They create a high-end semi-couture collection that creates the dream and the desire, which is very pricey and very few people have access to it. Then there's the part of the pyramid where you have a line of T-shirts or something that will give that flavor that still has the DNA of the brand. And the base of the pyramid is the fragrances and sunglasses and things that most people can access. I've noticed that even people who don't care about fashion still have, say a Burberry fragrance in their bathroom.

EM: Are after parties truly parties or are they business?

LM: New York City is a city moved by PR basically. A lot of the designers don't advertise, so their communication strategy is purely based on PR. A party is an opportunity to celebrate the end of a lot of work the designer put into a collection, but it's also an opportunity to invite more people. The show has the objective of inviting the buyers and press only. That's how it should be. People who need to write about it and who need to buy. Parties are a little more flexible.

EM: What was it like being in Naomi Campbell's Fashion for Relief show?

LM: It was very beautiful and emotional. It was a fundraiser to benefit Haiti so people were just excited to walk the runway. They were hugging and holding hands. It was beautiful.

EM: Any favorite moments from New York Fashion Week?

LM: Two seasons ago I took Lady Gaga to Marc's show. We arrived three minutes late so he had started. They didn't let us sit. I had to stand with the photographers. I looked over and saw Madonna watching the show too, and I just thought, "Wow." Music and fashion have always been related, but to have two of the biggest pop stars in one room looking at the biggest American designer felt very special.

Isaac Mizrahi

Kate Beckinsale and Pat McGrath

Anna Wintour

SNAPPED!

Mena Suvari

Jessica Stam and Catherine Holstein

Alexander Wang

SPRING/SUMMER
2010
A SPORTY SEASON
PRESENTED SEPTEMBER 12-17, 2009

TRENDS:
MAXIMAL MINIMALISM

TO THE EYE these clothes appeared minimal; however, a tremendous amount of detail had gone into them. Designers this season achieved one of the most difficult looks to achieve in fashion.

Marc Jacobs

Davidelfin

MILITARY

WITH THE WAR in Iraq still at full speed, designers couldn't help but be inspired by the military.

ACTIVE SPORT

TYPICALLY FOUND IN the gym, the athletic stripe found its way onto dresses, pants, etc.

Alexander Wang

Rachel Comey

SPRING/SUMMER 2010 **331**

Alexander Wang's side braid

Ralph Lauren's Americana

Marc Jacobs top knot

OTHER HIGHLIGHTS

Anna Sui's pink cheeks

Marchesa's dramatic silhouettes

ROGER AND MAURICIO PADILHA

Brothers Mauricio and Roger Padilha both had careers in the fashion industry before they joined forces to create MAO Public Relations. Mauricio graduated from Parsons School of Design and then went into PR. Roger was a designer and had success with his line, Spooky. The Padilha's gained acclaim by hosting MAO Space, an alternative venue for runway shows.

EILA MELL: What is a typical Fashion Week like for you?

MAURICIO PADILHA: Typically, we produce between seven and twelve events a season (one time we actually produced sixteen!). Fashion Week itself is pretty calm for us as by then we are fully organized and everything is in place for each event. It is the weeks leading up to it that are the craziest. Casting models, booking hair and makeup teams, inviting the press, working on seating charts, coordinating fittings, music selection, DJs. It is a lot to undertake for every show. The two weeks prior to Fashion Week, we are working till all hours of the night. It is stressful but also fun. You develop great camaraderie with your staff eating takeout at 3 AM.

EM: What goes into casting models for a show?

ROGER PADILHA: We typically see around three to four hundred models to cast eighteen girls in a show. We start by doing "go sees," where I meet each girl, look through their portfolios, and check out their walk. I photograph each girl and organize the pics into "Yes," "Maybe," and "No" folders on my computer. I then meet with each designer, talk about the spirit of the collection and what kind of girl they are envisioning. I usually show them just the models in the "Yes" and "Maybe" folders, get their feedback, and then I have to speak with agents to see if the selected girl's schedules and rates enable them to be in our show. It is exhausting but I love meeting new people and the whole mod-

eling process is still fascinating to me. The one thing that has changed as I get older is that I feel "fatherly" towards the girls, some of whom can be as young as fourteen. It is heartbreaking to meet these amazing young women and know in the back of my mind that I won't be giving 90 percent of them a job. You have to be completely objective, which gets harder for me each season.

EM: What role do parties play in Fashion Week?

MP: Unless you are a huge designer, like Marc Jacobs, who can get celebrities and the industry to go out of their way to attend his party, we tend to feel that after parties are a waste of time for most designers. The key people who you would want at a party (fashion editors, stylists, etc.) are so burned out from attending shows during the day that very few actually attend after parties. It usually ends up as a fun time for B-rate models and people not directly involved in Fashion Week (visual merchandisers of stores, sales people, etc.) or people not even in the industry but who want to take part in Fashion Week in some capacity. It is definitely not worth the time, effort, and expense for most designers.

EM: What do you think of the move to Lincoln Center?

RP: I think it is a very important move to establish New York Fashion Week as an important asset to New York City's image as well as a major revenue generator for the city. I still remember the days when designers would show out of their showrooms and there wasn't that much attention paid to Fashion Week, so the fact that it is in a venue as iconic as Lincoln Center is amazing. It is just another sign of how important the fashion industry has become.

EM: Who are the people you want in your audience or covering your shows?

MP: It really depends on the designer's customer. Of course every designer wants the editors of *Vogue*, style.com, and *The New York Times* to attend, but it really depends on the designer's price point and who is buying their clothes. We have some shows where a specific magazine or store would be front row and the very next day do a show where that same person is given a fourth- or fifth-row seat.

EM: Can you tell me about the runway shows at MAO Space?

RP: MAO Space came about when the tents at Bryant Park were first acquired by IMG. Previously, there was a very affordable space where young designers would be able to show but overnight that price tripled and most of the designers we had been producing shows for suddenly could not afford it. So we found a space, partnered with sponsors such as MAC Cosmetics, Creative Nail Design, Ian Schrager Hotels, and Red Bull, and created our own space. The price per designer was minimal and they received so many benefits from our sponsors. We showed for five seasons and had an amazing roster of young designers, including Peter Som, Doo.Ri, Gary Graham, Esteban Cortázar, and Patricia Field. It was amazing and really brought to light the need for affordable venues.

EM: Can you tell me about the Barbie show?

RP: For Barbie's fiftieth anniversary, we were contacted by Mattel to fully conceive and produce a fashion show like none other the industry had ever seen. We contacted fifty of the top American designers from Calvin Klein to Diane von Furstenberg to Donna Karan to design and construct a look that represented Barbie

to them. We created a hilarious ten-minute film which opened the show on huge plasma screens. The screens created the backdrop walls and then opened to reveal a chic, stylized dream house backdrop and the first model. We booked the top fifty models working that season and had Charlotte Tilbury and Orlando Pita do the hair and makeup. Everything was top notch and of course—pink! Everyone came. It got unbelievable press and was on every news channel the entire week. Barbie stole the spotlight from many of the designers that season.

EM: Roger, what was it like showing your own line, Spooky, for the first time?

RP: I believe it was for Spring 1994. I was given a timeslot during Absolut Fashion Week at the Palladium Night Club. It wasn't during regular Fashion Week so, to be honest, I didn't take it very seriously. I thought it would just be a fun way to introduce my new company to the downtown set. It was pretty campy with the first model, Nikki Uberti, walking out and spray painting the Spooky logo on the backdrop. But the next day, Jessica Kerwin wrote a full-page glowing review of it in *Women's Wear Daily* and that weekend Constance White from *The New York Times* did a huge article on it. It was overwhelming and overnight my label became the label to watch. From then on, we showed during New York Fashion Week proper and had a pretty good run for a while—until our backing ran out!

EM: What's the best part about working with the Blonds?

MP: The Blonds show is always super fun to do. Roger and I love their aesthetic and it allows us to be more theatrical than with other fashion shows. Where else can you suggest that one of the designers open the show in drag in a gorilla suit? Or to have a woman painted gold like Pussy Galore in *Goldfinger* swinging over the audience on a trapeze for the entire show? This might sound over the top but these are the types of shows that really bring excitement to our work as well as to New York Fashion Week. We have always sought out designers like this, whether it's Michael & Hushi, Sally LaPointe, or Heatherette. It showcases the energy of New York to the world.

EM: What are some of the more unusual things you've seen during New York Fashion Week?

RP: We've seen it all. From live animals on the runway to ego-driven drama cat fights between makeup artists and hairstylists to a thousand-person stampede which happened at our front of house at Bryant Park when the Phat Farm audience thought their ticket would ensure entry into the Baby Phat show. It's always unexpected. We have seen the best and worst of people during New York Fashion Week.

EM: What would people be surprised to know about New York Fashion Week?

RP: How at times it can be extremely boring! At the end of the day, Fashion Week is promoting business and it's not all fun and games.

FRESH FACES

PATRICIA VAN DER VLIET

FROM: THE NETHERLANDS | HEIGHT: 5'10½"
HAIR: BLONDE | EYES: BLUE

R'EL DADE

FROM: ALLEN, TEXAS | HEIGHT: 5'11½"
HAIR: BROWN | EYES: BROWN

THE SCENE

★ Anna Wintour and *Vogue* created Fashion's Night Out. The idea for the global event came out of the recession as a way to help designers and retailers whose businesses were suffering. With the help of CFDA president Diane von Furstenberg, the first annual event was held on September 10, 2009. Stores in countries all over the world stayed open until 11 PM to encourage people to shop. In New York City alone, more than seven hundred stores participated. Anna Wintour made an appearance at the Queens Center Mall; Victoria Beckham showed up at Bergdorf Goodman; and Oscar de la Renta sang with Bette Midler and Sarah Jessica Parker at his store in New York City. The crowd at Bergdorf's was so excited to see Mary-Kate and Ashley Olsen bartending that they knocked a door right off its hinges.

★ Fashion's Night Out was a major success, as stores were full of shoppers, many of whom bought a T-shirt designed for the event by Alexander Wang.

★ "I would like to give a big thank you to Anna Wintour for putting Fashion's Night Out together," said hairstylist Edward Tricomi. "She's made fashion fun in a different way and it's great for people to share the excitement. Fashion's Night Out made New York Fashion Week even more exciting and bigger."

★ Richard Chai introduced his new line, Richard Chai Love. The designer unveiled this lower-priced collection at his September 12 show at the Cedar Lake ballet studio.

★ Courtney Love and Santigold performed at Alexander Wang's after party, which was held at the Mobil gas station at Milk Studios. Guests, including actress Kirsten Dunst, Anna Wintour's daughter Bee Shaffer, and model Devon Aoki were treated to cheeseburgers from Pop Burger. The guests were free to help themselves to whatever they wanted from the gas station's convenience store. Some worried that people were smoking by the gas pumps, but there was no danger as the gas had been turned off long before the party began.

★ Thirteen-year-old blogger Tavi Gevinson came from Chicago to New York Fashion Week. She was one of many bloggers covering the shows. In addition to bloggers, a large number of guests reported the goings on of the week on Twitter.

★ Y-3's Spring 2010 show ended with a net coming onto the runway. Models Irina Lazareanu, Heloise Guerin, Vlada Roslyakova, Katrin Thormann, Sheila Marquez, and Naty Chabanenko, armed with soccer balls, took shots at a goal. They were followed by designer Yohji Yamamoto and French World Cup winner Zinedine Zidane. Zidane took his own shot as the crowd cheered.

★ Isaac Mizrahi's Spring 2010 collection was inspired by 1950s Gene Kelly films. To that end, his set included klieg lights and a wind machine to evoke the feeling of an old studio lot. In a very *Singin' in the Rain* moment, a male escort equipped with an umbrella walked models under a rain machine in the middle of the runway. As if that wasn't enough, Mizrahi's show also featured a golf cart and a staircase for the models to navigate, making this one of the most dramatic shows of the season.

Yoko Ono

Issac Mizrahi

Lorenzo Martone and Allison Sarofim

SNAPPED!

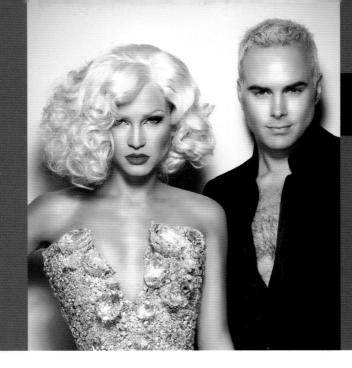

THE BLONDS

Phillipe and David Blond met in New York City. Phillipe was born in Puerto Rico, raised in New York, and studied design at the Fashion Institute of Technology. David, originally from Key West, studied Fashion Merchandising and Design at the International Fine Arts College in Miami. He dressed windows and interiors for Macy's Herald Square and Saks Fifth Avenue. The Blonds have specially made pieces for Fergie, Madonna, Katy Perry, Rihanna, Shakira, Britney Spears, Kylie Minogue, etc.

EILA MELL: What was it like showing your collection for the first time?

THE BLONDS: A dream come true! The rush of excitement is always overwhelming when you do anything for the first time and this was tenfold. All our friends and family were there to support us, including one of Phillipe's idols, Christian Louboutin. He provided the footwear and sat in the front row!

EM: Do you have a favorite collection?

TB: Collections are like children and each piece is another baby.

EM: What do you think of the move to Lincoln Center?

TB: Lincoln Center is a major center for the arts in New York City. Adding Fashion Week to it is like the frosting on the cake—red velvet of course.

EM: What are some of your memories from New York Fashion Week?

TB: Meeting Christian Louboutin, having Barbie walk in the show, and Phillipe transforming from a gorilla into a goddess.

EM: What was it like designing for Barbie?

TB: Total dream come true. She's the ultimate fantasy client!

EM: What was your breakthrough as designers?

TB: Dressing Beyoncé.

EM: What's the most fun part of Fashion Week?

TB: Our show, and the after party, of course.

EM: What do you look for in models?

TB: Extreme looks and girls that can walk in the tallest Louboutins and the tightest corsets!

EM: How do you balance both the creative and business aspects of your work?

TB: This is probably one of the hardest parts of being a young designer. If you're not business minded then you better learn fast!

EM: Do you have a signature piece?

TB: The corset.

EM: From a business point of view, is it important to have celebrities wear your clothing?

TB: Extremely important because they are part of our clientele and also support the business through the press they bring.

EM: How do you select the music for a show?

TB: We work with Mr. Wilson and usually send him what we've been listening to while making the collection. He'll then pull together something amazing and incorporate the feeling we want to evoke. Our shows are meant to be a total sensory overload and transport you into another dimension. A Blonds show is an escape into a world where everything is possible, fabulous, and glamorous!

EM: What would people be surprised to know about New York Fashion Week?

TB: There is a tremendous amount of work that goes into producing Fashion Week. It's 99 percent perspiration and 1 percent inspiration. You have to love this business to survive, and we do.

SNAPPED!

Ralph Rucci

Tommy Hilfiger

Mickey Boardman and Lyn Yeager

Rachel Comey, model: Kelly Moreira

FALL/WINTER
2010
MAD MEN MANIA
PRESENTED FEBRUARY 11–18, 2010

TRENDS:
1950s
HOURGLASS

STYLES INSPIRED BY the hit television show *Mad Men* were abundant as we saw a resurgence of the classic silhouette of the femme fatale.

Milly

Marc Jacobs

MAN
TAILORED

THERE WAS A return to tailoring as designers offered up suits inspired by Jon Hamm's Don Draper character for female customers.

FUR

THERE WAS FUR on many runways; both real and faux.

Brian Reyes

Thakoon

Prabal Gurung

THE SCENE

★ The death of Alexander McQueen shocked and deeply saddened the fashion industry. McQueen took his own life days after losing his beloved mother, Joyce. McQueen's death occurred on the first day of New York Fashion Week and was on everyone's minds at the tents.

★ Naomi Campbell's Fashion for Relief show started with Sarah Ferguson acknowledging McQueen, and ended with a poignant tribute on the runway. Daphne Guinness came out wearing McQueen's designs, and was followed by Helena Christensen, Natasha Poly, Karen Elson, Amber Valletta, Sasha Pivovarova, and Campbell, also dressed in Alexander McQueen.

★ Rock legend Patti Smith played the LnA party at Milk Studios, and dedicated her last song to McQueen.

★ *Harper's Bazaar* introduced the Front Row, a series of short videos chronicling Fashion Weeks in New York, Paris, and Milan. The videos covered everything from the runway to the after parties.

★ It was no longer necessary to have an invitation to see a show. Top labels, such as Marc Jacobs, Alexander Wang, and Calvin Klein streamed their shows live on the Internet, making fashion shows accessible to a universal audience.

★ Calvin Klein had 1990s top models Stella Tennant, Kristen McMenamy, Kirsty Hume, and Tanga Moreau walk the Fall 2010 runway.

★ Robert Duffy (of Marc Jacobs) asked people for ideas for the set design for Jacobs' Fall show via Twitter.

★ Marc Jacobs' after party was strictly for employees this season.

★ Fall 2010 marked the debut of Sarah Jessica Parker as president and chief creative officer of Halston.

★ Demi Moore had a front-row seat at Donna Karan's show. The actress was particularly taken with one look and asked to wear it to a screening of her film *Happy Tears* the following day. Karan, who was a co-host of the screening and a longtime friend of Moore's, said yes.

★ Donna Karan's show marked her collection's twenty-fifth anniversary.

★ Sophie Theallet showed her first collection since winning the CFDA/*Vogue* Fashion Fund award. The award entitles the winning designer to $200,000 as well as a team of business mentors. The CFDA/*Vogue* Fashion Fund was created to help emerging designers. "Vogue has really encouraged new talent," said Candy Pratts Price, creative director for vogue.com. "Designers like Marc Jacobs aren't going to be here forever. *Vogue* and the CFDA did something about it and found new designers."

★ Tommy Hilfiger's was the last show ever to be presented at Bryant Park. After his bow, Hilfiger made an emotional speech, and acknowledged Fern Mallis and Stan Herman, who brought the idea of the Bryant Park tents to fruition in 1993.

Rachel Zoe

Alexander McQueen

Brooke Shields, Demi Moore, and Susan Sarandon

TOMMY HILFIGER

Tommy Hilfiger has designed clothes under the Tommy label since 1984. He has designed menswear, women's wear, children's wear, denim, footwear, fragrances, accessories, and home furnishings. He was awarded the From the Catwalk to the Sidewalk award at the first VH1 Fashion and Music Awards, and was named the 1995 Menswear Designer of the Year by the CFDA.

EILA MELL: What was your first season showing at New York Fashion week like?

TOMMY HILFIGER: Our first menswear collection in 1985 will always have a special place in my heart. I designed the collection for men like myself, who wanted preppy American sportswear, then I added a twist.

EM: Your twenty-fifth anniversary fashion show was such a special event. What can you tell me about it?

TH: I really wanted to thank everyone for their support over the past twenty-five years. The entire evening, beginning with my show and ending with the Strokes performing at the Metropolitan Opera was beyond my wildest dreams. I loved every minute of it.

EM: Your show closed the Bryant Park era. Was that an emotional evening?

TH: Closing Bryant Park was bittersweet because it had been such a great home to the fashion industry, but at the same time change is good. I have wonderful memories of Bryant Park but I am also thrilled that the shows are now at Lincoln Center.

EM: There were seasons when you chose to not show at Bryant Park. What went into that decision, and why did you choose to return?

TH: For years we were re-establishing our runway presence in iconic, off-site venues such as Lincoln Center. But I love showing in the tents. The energy is incredible and it's great to support the fashion industry.

EM: Opening your Fifth Avenue store must have been a landmark occasion.

TH: The Fifth Avenue store is a homecoming for the brand. It is an incredible feeling to have the largest Tommy Hilfiger retail store worldwide finally in the city where we launched the brand twenty-five years ago.

EM: Is there a particular piece or season you've designed that stands out as a favorite?

TH: My first collection. It was comfortable, casual clothes with unexpected details. I'll never forget what an adrenaline rush it was to show for the very first time.

EM: Your shows are always one of the hottest tickets. What role do you play in deciding who gets an invitation?

TH: It takes a lot of teamwork to plan a fashion show, and I always like to make sure that my family and friends are there so we can share the experience.

EM: How do you balance being both a creative and business person?

TH: You have to stay true to your roots, stay true to yourself, and work hard. I am always looking for new ways to challenge myself and learn more.

EM: How do you think the move to Lincoln Center will affect New York Fashion Week?

TH: The move will be a fresh take on an old tradition, and that should be fun for everyone. I think that change after a while is always a good thing, especially moving to a place like Lincoln Center. It's an iconic institution that offers sophistication and culture unlike any other.

FRESH FACE

NEW ON THE SCENE

THE ROW

Fashion icons Mary-Kate and Ashley Olsen had their first ever runway show for their three-year-old label.

BONNIE CHEN

FROM: NANJING, JIANGSU, CHINA | HEIGHT: 5'10" | HAIR: BLACK | EYES: BROWN

LAQUAN SMITH

LaQuan Smith was born in Queens, New York. He began his career in fashion as an intern at *Blackbook* magazine. Smith started his eponymous brand in 2008. His career took off when he created custom pieces for Lady Gaga, Rhianna, and Beyoncé. LaQuan Smith received the F.O.C.U.S. for Life Service award for surviving cancer and not letting the trauma of such an experience hold him back from his passion.

"LaQuan Smith is a wave of the future for fashion. As a young, self-taught American designer, he has visionary skills with technique and dressmaking that is parallel to some of the greatest world-class designers who have shaped modern fashion." —André Leon Talley

EILA MELL: How did you get your Fall 2010 show off the ground?

LAQUAN SMITH: I got it off the ground with the help of all my friends, family, and the team at the Fashion Art Gallery. Kelly Mills of Fashion Art was able to arrange the space at the Society of Illustrators, the sponsors, the layout, and the press involved. I made the collection with the financial support of my family and friends and I truly appreciate their help. I was so proud when I was able to finally showcase my work to the world.

EM: You have such wonderful supporters, especially André Leon Talley. How has that helped you in your career?

LQS: Within the fashion community my major supporters and most recent influencers include André Leon Talley, Tyra Banks, and Diane von Furstenberg. André has opened his mind to my world and has allowed me to dream further than I ever have before. He has given me expert advice, personal advice, true mentoring, and friendship.

EM: Do you have a signature piece?

LQS: I wouldn't say that I have a signature piece but I have my idea of the LaQuan Smith woman. She is the personification of modernity, sensuality, and liberation in femininity. I don't want to have a staple just yet. I like the element of surprise. I feel my designs are for all women and I shall have further insight as I grow in this ever-evolving industry.

EM: Do you feel you have the opportunity to grow, or do you feel you're expected to perform as well as veterans?

LQS: It is exhilarating to be a new designer. There are endless new doors that open up in front of you, new opportunities, and new experiences. Personally, I feel as though I am given the opportunity to grow, but because the whole industry is always changing and always moving on to the next hot thing, you have to mature at a rapid rate. The competition is very steep in the industry and there is always a fresh-faced designer waiting to take your place.

EM: What do you love most about your job?

LQS: What I love most is that I am able to design, create, and showcase my own fashion perspective. I am allowed the full creative control to demonstrate my idea of what should be the newest trend in women's fashion.

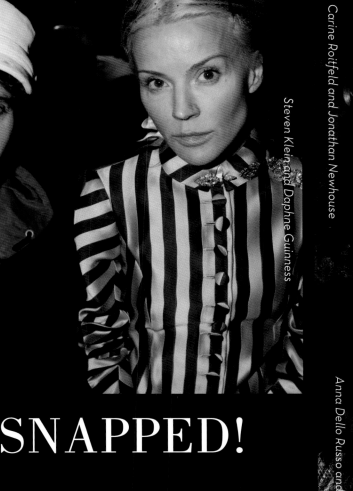

Steven Klein and Daphne Guinness

Carine Roitfeld and Jonathan Newhouse

SNAPPED!

Anna Dello Russo and Olivier Zahm

Yohji Yamamoto

Justin Timberlake and Trace Ayala

Malandrino

SPRING/SUMMER
2011
A NEW HOME
PRESENTED SEPTEMBER 9-16, 2010

TRENDS:
1970s SLOUCHY MAXI

VINTAGE HALSTON MIXED with 1970s bohemian created the slouchy maxi for Spring 2011. Worn with flats, these dresses went everywhere from day to evening.

Badgley Mischka

Alexander Wang

NEUTRALS

IT WAS AN anti-black, ivory tower season. There were shades of soft cream, beige, greige, white, and off-white on most runways.

GRAPHICS

Jeremy Scott

Z Spoke by Zac Posen

Popluxe

ANDRÉ LEON TALLEY

North Carolina-native André Leon Talley graduated from Brown University with a master's degree in French. In 1975 he went to work for Andy Warhol's *Interview* magazine, where he answered phones mostly, but also covered fashion shows. Warhol introduced Talley to the legendary Diana Vreeland, who impacted his life significantly. André Leon Talley joined *Vogue* magazine in 1983, and has remained for more than twenty-five years. He is the author of *A.L.T.: A Memoir* and serves as a judge on *America's Next Top Model*.

EILA MELL: You've championed and helped nurture some of the best new designers in the industry. What do you look for in someone new that makes you want to get behind them?

ANDRÉ LEON TALLEY: I always look for a sense of humility and true talent. A young designer can often make horrible garments, but if they have the finesse of workmanship, and a sense of confidence, it resonates upon my hard drive.

EM: How has New York Fashion Week evolved since the start of the Bryant Park years?

ALT: New York Fashion Week has finally come to a home, Lincoln Center, that gives not only the professional audiences a sense of well-being, but the very actors on stage—designers, lighting technicians, models, and backstage workers—a place that feels as if one is really in a world of culture and refinement.

André and Sarah Ferguson at Fashion for Relief Hurricane Katrina Show

FRESH FACES

ARIZONA MUSE

FROM: SANTA FE, NEW MEXICO
HEIGHT: 5'10" | HAIR: BLONDE
EYES: GREEN

HAILEY CLAUSON

FROM: CALIFORNIA | HEIGHT: 5'11"
HAIR: BLONDE | EYES: BLUE

THE SCENE

★ The big news this season was New York Fashion Week's move to Lincoln Center, which incorporates four show locations—the Theatre, the Stage, the Studio, and the Box Presentation Space. Stephanie Winston Wolkoff, formerly of *Vogue*, was brought in as fashion director for Lincoln Center.

★ Two days before the first show of the season, Lincoln Center held the largest public fashion show ever. Called Fashion's Night Out: The Show, the proceedings were streamed live on the Internet, where it was hosted by André Leon Talley and model-turned-blogger Hanneli Mustaparta. More than two hundred models wore fashions from numerous designers, which were already in stores. The evening served as a lead in for the second annual Fashion's Night Out.

★ The second annual Fashion's Night Out took place on September 10, 2010. Model Karlie Kloss participated in Barney's New York karaoke contest, judged by Mary-Kate and Ashley Olsen, Proenza Schouler designers Jack McCullough and Lazaro Hernandez, and model Liya Kebede. CBS documented the goings on around New York and other cities for a documentary called *The Making of Fashion's Night Out*, which debuted four nights later.

★ Perhaps one of the most talked-about shows was Tom Ford's. This was the designer's first women's show since 2004. Except for Terry Richardson, Ford did not allow anyone to take pictures of his collection. He also would not release any photos to the media before December, a precaution to guard against overexposure before his clothes went into stores.
  Ford personally announced each model and spoke about the designs they were wearing. The designer chose models of all ages and body types, including Beyoncé, Lauren Hutton, Marisa Berenson, Julianne Moore, Karlie Kloss, Rita Wilson, and Stella Tennant.

★ Tommy Hilfiger's show marked the designer's twenty-fifth year in fashion. Afterwards, guests such as Jennifer Lopez, Neil Patrick Harris, and Lenny Kravitz celebrated at the Metropolitan Opera House, where they were entertained by the Strokes.

★ The Row designers, Mary-Kate and Ashley Olsen, cancelled their scheduled runway show due to late deliveries. The designers announced that they would be showing during Paris Fashion Week.

★ Alexander Wang held his after party at the Edison parking lot in New York City. He transformed the space into a carnival, with skee ball, bumper cars, and a carousel.

★ Tara Subkoff showed at New York Fashion Week for the first time in five years. Her Imitation of Christ line was now simply called Imitation.

★ Zac Posen debuted a lower-priced line called Z Spoke by Zac Posen.

★ One of Fashion Week's best kept secrets was the appearance of Ellen DeGeneres in Richie Rich's Popluxe show. Many thought that DeGeneres was the designer when she first appeared on the runway, clad in a suit with a Popluxe T-shirt underneath. Seconds later the audience realized it was DeGeneres, and soon after, Rich finally came out to greet the audience. The pair amused the crowd with their over-the-top stroll down the runway. The moment was one of the highlights of the week.

Richie Rich and Ellen DeGeneres

David Blond, Selita Ebanks, and Phillipe Blond

Marc Jacobs and Courtney Love

RICHIE RICH

Former club kid Richie Rich burst onto the scene as one half of the design duo Heatherette. Rich and co-designer Traver Rains created whimsical runway shows that were crowd favorites. In 2010 Rich debuted his new line, Popluxe, at New York Fashion Week at Lincoln Center. No stranger to theatricality, Rich has appeared in the film *Zoolander* and on the television shows *Project Runway*, *Paris Hilton's My New BFF*, and *America's Next Top Model*.

EILA MELL: How did you like showing your new line, Popluxe, at Lincoln Center?

RICHIE RICH: It was really super fun and generous of them to let me open it that night. I had a great time. I opened the show with ballerinas and violinists because of the move to Lincoln Center. This was our first outing with the new line. I was happy with it. I feel like everyone walked away with a smile and hopefully some confetti.

EM: What are some of your influences as a designer?

RR: I was a skater in *Ice Capades*. I think my ice-skating roots make me want to make it more theatrical, to have that bridge over the gap of dullness. I love designers who have inspired me in the past, like Westwood and Mugler. A lot of times when I show it's not just buyers and editors. I like when non-fashion people can open their eyes to a new world. I get to de-virginize a lot of fashionistas. That's always fun.

EM: How do you decide on the hair and makeup for a show?

RR: The hair and makeup always reflect where the collection comes from, whether it's *Breakfast at Tiffany's*, Marilyn Monroe, or *The Wizard of Oz*.

EM: What was your first Bryant Park experience?

RR: When I moved to New York in the 1990s I really had no idea about the tents. A friend of mine dragged me to the Todd Oldham show. We didn't have tickets so we just crashed it. Now when kids try to get into my shows I let them—I was that kid. We had standing room at Todd Oldham. My eyes were opened at that show. It was like Broadway. Todd really inspired me.

EM: You've had socialite Tinsley Mortimer walk in some of your shows.

RR: I've known Tinsley for a while. When she walked in my first Heatherette show in Bryant Park she wanted to be really punky with this big prom dress on. The bigger the hair the better; she looked amazing. Everybody expected her to walk for someone like Oscar de la Renta. We had a blast. If there's ever a really good charity I'll call her and she'll be there. She's a good girl.

EM: What's the difference between Heatherette and Popluxe?

RR: There's definitely a parallel to Heatherette in Popluxe because it all comes from my crazy brain. My brain's like a box of crayons but I took out the gray. Basically I think Popluxe is more wearable and available. Heatherette eventually sold at Macy's and Bloomingdale's and other great stores. I want Popluxe to be available for those who want it. My hands are more on this collection. I'm learning as I go. It's like fashion school backwards.

EM: How did you get started in fashion?

RR: I was a club kid and I went all over the world. I always assisted people during the day. I never wanted to sleep all day, get up, and go to the clubs. I never got into the drug scene, luckily. I just wanted to look pretty. Luckily I met [event producer] Susanne Bartsch and assisted her. She took me everywhere and introduced me to everyone. I was fresh off the glitter boat. I was making clothes for my friends all along.

Eventually, Susanne saw what I was doing. She suggested I bring my clothes to Patricia Field to sell. Pat saw a shirt I did where I put my name, Richie, in rhinestones. She said to make that shirt for Carrie. I didn't know who Carrie was, but it turned out to be Carrie Bradshaw from *Sex and the City*. Pat was the show's costume designer.

Susanne told me to take Polaroids of my T-shirts, put them on a piece of paper, and show my friends. I started doing that. I didn't know I was doing a line sheet; I didn't even know what that was. I showed it to David LaChapelle. He brought me to one of his favorite stylists, Patti Wilson, who he was working with. She and David were shooting Karolina Kurkova for *Vanity Fair* the next day, and she asked me to do the wardrobe. I had gotten my friend Traver Rains into assisting me before he became my design partner. We stayed up all night and made a dress. We showed up at 7 AM and Patti said, "Where's the rest of the clothes?" I said, "This is it!"

David was really instrumental in how Heatherette really came about. He said, "Go back to your place and gather all your bits and bobs and baubles and stick it in a suitcase and bring that airbrush machine I saw you making T-shirts with." So we packed it all up, and from about 7 AM to 2 AM the next morning we created clothes on Karolina. We did the cover of *Look*, *I-D*, and *Vanity Fair*. It was really super fun. David compared it to the Warhol Factory. The next day Steven Tyler called because he saw the *Sex and the City* stuff. Missy Elliott called, Lil Kim called, Gwen Stefani called, Mariah Carey called . . .

EM: What was your first show at Bryant Park like?

RR: The first show was Rock and Roll High School. We felt like the misfits, like we didn't belong in the tents. We had Lydia Hearst walking with this fabulous Asian model, holding hands like lesbians. She was smoking a cigarette. Paris Hilton came out in a Jem and the Holograms dress. Super fun. Then Amanda Lepore came out to Rock and Roll High School. She was checking her watch, but she didn't have one on! She was in a corset with heels and everyone wondered what she was doing. She was stalling for time because Naomi Campbell had to make her way over from the VH1 Music Awards. We dressed her as she ran from her car.

EM: How did you get Naomi Campbell for your first show?

RR: I met her through Steven Klein and Patti Wilson. Naomi called one day. I thought it was my friend Tobell so I hung up on her. She called back. I said, "Tobell, stop it. I'm busy." She said, "It's Naomi. You're coming to my house. Bring some dresses. I'm going to the MTV awards." She sent us a car twenty minutes later. We played dress up. She taught me so much in that one half hour of fun. I whispered in her ear, "If you walked in our show it'd be amazing." She found out when it was and showed up! I found out five minutes before she came. Those are the moments in fashion that are really fun.

EM: One of the most fun surprises of the Spring 2011 shows was Ellen DeGeneres's surprise appearance on the Popluxe runway. How did that come about?

RR: She called two days before the show. We weren't allowed to tell anybody. She was just great, couldn't be better. She's a new muse to me.

SNAPPED!

Catherine Malandrino and Hamish Bowles

Michael Kors and Brana Wolf

Patrick Demarchelier and Fabien Baron

FERN MALLIS

Fern Mallis was named the executive director of the CFDA in 1991. She is known as the originator of New York Fashion Week as we now know it, as she organized the shows in the centralized location of Bryant Park. When the duties of hosting Fashion Week went to IMG, Mallis went too, and she stayed with the company until 2010.

EILA MELL: It was your idea to have New York Fashion Week in one centralized location. What was it like for you that first day at the tents?

FERN MALLIS: It was extraordinary. It was a magical time to see something like that absolutely get pulled off with all these major designers there. We created systems that are in place now that never existed before; from credentials and press, to organizing a guest list, to organizing a sponsor handbook. One season led to the next season and the next. Everybody all grew together as an industry.

EM: What was the relationship like with the Bryant Park board?

FM: I think the first half of the years they loved having us there, but I also think they felt they never got the credit they deserved for the park being so fabulous. The early configuration of the tents was much more unfriendly to the city than the final configuration on the lawn. Once we were off the plazas and on the lawn the park was open and accessible. It integrated beautifully with the energy on the street. Everyone in New York knew it was Fashion Week. It was a marvelous partnership for a long time.

EM: Why the move to Chelsea Piers then for Spring/Summer 1998?

FM: There was tension at the park with the restaurant operators. Bryant Park Grill felt it was hurting their business to have a tent in front of their restaurant. Most people said, "Are you crazy? How could having thousands of people in the park every day, and models and celebrities hurt your restaurant?" So it was really one of those seasons of calling their bluff in a way. We said, "Fine. We'll move it." And I actually think that the venues at Chelsea Piers were some of the best we ever had. General Motors was a sponsor then so we had fleets of cars on site. If anybody needed to get anywhere they were just waiting at the doors. It was marvelous, but the press hated it. Others said they didn't want to cross a highway in stilettos. At that point many of the off-site shows started to happen and they were all in Chelsea. They were a block away and nobody minded going to those. It's not easy moving the industry around. But that's when Mayor Giuliani said take the lawn and come back to Bryant Park.

EM: What do you think of the shows being streamed on the web?

FM: Well you know, a few years ago IMG did that, before anybody else did. There was a whole season where every show was streamed live around the world. I think on one hand anything that promotes fashion and gets it out there is great. On the other hand, I think the fashion industry is finding itself at a crossroads, trying to figure out who the shows are for. You know, is it consumer; is it trade; is it exclusive. I don't know that they've come up with the answers yet.

EM: Fashion has emerged into the mainstream. Do you think shows like *Project Runway* are responsible for that?

FM: I think *Project Runway* had a huge influence on fashion, but I think it made every kid who can sew two pieces of fabric together think they can be a designer. Fashion began emerging into the mainstream before *Project Runway*. It used to be that you got your information from *The New York Times* and *Women's Wear Daily*. All of a sudden there were thousands registered as press, all of them sending messages out. Hundreds of thousands of people have a Blackberry or a computer and a camera. Everybody's a reporter and everybody's a critic. It has completely changed. Before all that people didn't know who most of the designers were.

EM: The media reported that when the European designers started to show here the American designers were upset. Is that true?

FM: Absolutely. When we gave Gianni Versace the first opening night slot a lot of designers were really upset and said it wasn't fair; it was about America, the tents were created for American designers. I said that America is the melting pot of the world, which makes New York Fashion Week the Ellis Island of fashion. That's how a foreign designer can gain exposure to the American marketplace. I said, "Gianni can show here, and he's bringing a plane load full of Italian journalists who might not otherwise show up in New York, and you're going to benefit from that. And he's going to help put us on the map so you have to embrace this."

EM: America used to show after Europe. Why was the decision made for us to show first?

FM: That was a pretty horrifying season. Helmut Lang moved his business to America. He was probably one of the most directional designers in the world. Editors and the press would go anywhere to see him. He decided one day that he wanted to show in New York, and he didn't want to wait until Europe did their calendar for whatever reason. So other designers said if he was going to show they would show the same week. Then Calvin Klein called me and said, "You're going to kill me, but I think I'm going to show when Helmut's showing." And then obviously the industry met, we got everybody together, and decided we could go first. That was the shift. Prior to that, the shows were presented in early October. After Europe ended there was a week for people to get their orders in Europe, for photo shoots to happen, and then come back.

EM: Lastly, I heard you modeled for a show?

FM: I wouldn't say modeled! I walked in a show that Yeohlee did. She always did shows that were off the beaten path, whether it was the location on a subway or somewhere. She often used real people and I was one of the real people. It was fun because when I came out the door and turned the corner and everybody saw me their reaction was wonderful. Everybody was just clapping and screaming, and the photographers! It was amazing. They all made me feel like a million dollars.

The power of fashion is that it can make anyone feel like a million dollars.

INDEX

A

Abbound, Joseph, 283
Absolutely Fabulous, 185
Adrover, Miguel, 56, *163*
Aguiar, James, 117, *117*, 119
Alaïa, Azzedine, 268
Alba, Jessica, 306
Alexander, Hilary, 251
Alexander, J., *17*
Alfaro, Victor, *153*
Allure, 78, 107
A.L.T.: A Memoir, 354
Alt, Carol, 55
Altman, Robert, 129
Altuzarra, Joseph, *314*
Ambrosio, Alessandra, 325
American Idol, 129
America's Most Smartest Model, 128
America's Next Top Model, 17, 98, 354, 358
Annan, Kofi, 126
Aoki, Devon, 336
Aoki, Miho, 233
Aouad, Gabrielle Rich, 155
Aouad, Philip, 155
Argiro, Kathlin, 155
Armani, Giorgio, 26, *106*, *106*, 107
Arover, Miguel, 229
AsFour, 239, 261, 284, 322
Astley, Amy, 251
Aubry, Gabriel, *174*
Aucoin, Kevyn, 55, 65
Avedon, Richard, 218
Ayala, Trace, *349*
Azria, Max, 175, 307, 313, 315
Azrouël, Yigal, 303, *303*, 321

B

Baby Phat, 208, 239, 251, 335
Bacall, Lauren, 186
Bailey, David, 36
Bailey, Glenda, *46*, *46*
Balenciaga, 36, 37, *172*, *174*, 175, 187, 315
Balti, Bianca, *234*
Banks, Tyra, *12*, 129, 348
Barbie show, *320*, 334, 338
Barcelona, Custo, 175, *236*
Baron, Fabien, 360
Barrows, Sydney Biddle, 175
Bartlett, John, *154*
Bartley, Luella, 175
Bartsch, Susanne, 359
Basco, 33
Bassmon, Lillian, 251
Basso, Dennis, 283
Battaglia, Giovanna, 164
Bax, Kylie, *77*
BCBG Max Azria, 175, 313, 315
Be Eco Chic Show, *312*
Beckford, Tyson, *252*
Beckham, Victoria, *297*, 336
Beckinsale, Kate, *326*
Beckman, Narc, 229
Beene, Geoffrey, *14*, 34, 37, 43, 147, 198, 286, 304
Behind the Label, 117

Behind the Music, 129
Behind the Velvet Rope, 196
Belafonte, Harry, 239, *239*
Bennett, Chuck, 175
Bennett, Laura, *273*
Benz, Chris, 272, *277*
Berenson, Marisa, *49*, 356
Bergdorf Goodman, 117, 262, 304, 336
Berkova, Marleen, *150*
Berman, Barbara, 24, *24*
Bernhard, Sandra, 148, 254
Bessette, Carolyn, 72, 76
Beyoncé, 118, 210, 239, 245, 252, 338, 356
Bittar, Marcelle, *179*
Bjork, *27*
Bjornson, Karen, 210, *211*
Blahnik, Manolo, 274
Blaine, David, 229
Blair, Selma, *163*
Blass, Bill, 7, 23, 30, 37, 40, 61, 94, 125, *135*, *135*, 147, *163*, 195, 210, 259, 260
Blige, Mary J., 261, 265
Bloch, Phillip, 26, *26*, 147, *163*
Blond, David, 338, *357*
Blond, Phillipe, 338, *357*
Bloomberg, Michael, 175, 217, 229, 321
Blow, Isabella, 64, *64*
Boardman, Mickey, *339*
Bond Girl, 126
Bond, James, 126
Bono, *307*
Bouwer, Marc, 149, 175, 303, 321
Bowen, Anne, 34
Bowie, David, 251
Bowles, Hamish, 360
Boy George, 135, 242
Bradley, Bryan, 210
Brandy, *91*
Breytenbach, Nicola, *146*
British Marie Claire, 46
British Vogue, 107, 196, 274
Brooks, Ridgely, 244
Brown, James, 271
Brown, Ryan, 325
B-Rude, 239, *242*, 251
Broderick, Matthew, *297*
Bruni, Carla, 23, 39
Bryant Park, 7, 10, 13, 15, 16, 24, 26, 33, 37, 55, 68, 78, 86, 89, 90, 96, 106, 117, 126, 128, 136, 148, 156, 169, 171, 176, 195, 207, 241, 244, 254, 255, 271, 294, 321, 334, 335, 344, 346, 354, 358, 359, 361
Buchanan, Pat, 64
Buck, Sibyl, *92*
Bullock, Sandra, 26
Bündchen, Gisele, *139*, 147, *155*, 175, *214*, 215
Burch, Tory, 255, 271
Burmeister, Lars, 232
Burrows, Stephen, 210, *228*, 229
Bush, Laura, 239, 283, 303

C

Callaghan, 155
Campbell, Naomi, 6, 7, 16, 45, 62, 129, 130, 187, *189*, 229, 236, 252, *252*, 255, 294, 296, 326, 344, 359
Cañadas, Esther, *79*, *104*, *122*
Cannon, 79
Carey, Mariah, 359
Cargo, 222
Carrilero, Pierre, *189*
Castillo, Edmundo, 164, *164*
Cavaco, Paul, 210
Cha, Rosa, 34, 210
Chabanenko, Naty, 336
Chai, Richard, 336
Chaiken, Julie, 261
Chanel, 17, 65, 107, 197, 215
Chang, Don, 294
Chang, Jin, 294
Chapman, Georgina, 302, 307
Chen, Bonnie, *347*
Chen, Shiatzy, 65
Chicago, 207
Child, 241
Chloe, 82
Choay, Coline, *314*
Choo, Jimmy, 303
Chow, China, 195
Christensen, Helena, 23, *43*, 85, 344
Chung, Doo.Ri, *198*, *310*, 334
Chung, Jane, 115
Cianfarani, Atom, 149
ck, *12*
Claiborne, Liz, 75, *75*
Clarke, Imogen Morris, *314*
Clarke, Jeff, 315
Clarke, Mary, 315
Clauson, Hailey, 355
Clemente, Chiara, 303
Cleveland, Pat, 210, *211*
Clinton, Bill, 6
Clinton, Chelsea, 135
Clinton, Hillary, 155
Cochran, Johnnie, *168*
Coddington, Grace, 307
Cole, Kenneth, 155, *163*, *194*, 205, 206, 217, 222, 237, 251
Coler, Jack R., 229
Colovos, Michael, 294, *295*
Colovos, Nicole, 294, *295*
Combs, Janice, 168
Combs, Sean, 195
Comey, Rachel, 322, *331*, 340
Committed: A Rabble-Rouser's Memoir, 148
Conran, Jasper, 65
Copperfield, David, 45
Coppola, Sofia, 23, *23*
Cortázar, Esteban, 210, 217, 334
Cosmopolitan, 78, 107
Costa, Francisco, 210, *211*
Costello, Jeffrey, 231, *313*
Cota, Christian, 56
Countdown with Keith Olbermann, 129
Couric, Katie, 229
Craig, Keren, 307
Crawford, Cindy, 6, 7, *11*, 45, 99, *125*, *125*, 210, *211*, 255

Crow, Sheryl, *264*
CSI: NY, 218
Cumming, Alan, *125, 125, 163,* 313
Cunanan, Andrew, 96
Cuomo, Mario, 155
Cushnie et Ochs, *310*
Custo Barcelona, 105
Cutrone, Kelly, *321, 322,* 322

D

Daily Show with Jon Stewart, The, 129, 155
Daily Telegraph, 251
Dalmau, Custo, *105, 105*
Dalmau, David, *105*
Damhave, Matt, 157
Danes, Claire, 76
Daryl K, 86, 96, *134,* 155
Davidelfin, *330*
de Castro, Max, *321*
de la Renta, Oscar, 7, 15, 22, 26, 80, 103, 107,
    118, *122, 123,* 130, *132,* 134, 147, *152, 154,*
    155, 164, *172,* 204, *206,* 210, 244, 253, *271,*
    302, 315, 336, 358
De Niro, Robert, *297*
Deal, Donald, *124*
Dean, Howard, 210
DeGeneres, Ellen, *356, 357,* 359
Dell'Orrefice, Carmen, *175*
Demarchelier, Patrick, 107, *284,* 360
Demsey, John, 229
Deschanel, Zooey, *283, 287*
Desert Flower, 126
Desperate Housewives, 254
Destiny's Child, 251
Devil Wears Prada, The, 118, 136
Deyn, Agyness, 275
Dicker, Cintia, *221,* 251
Dickinson, Janice, 251
DiGeronimo, Stephen, 13
Dinkins, David, 7, 13
Dinkins, Joyce, 13
Dior, Christian, 65
Dirie, Waris, *126, 126*
DKNY, *10,* 13, 18, *20, 21,* 32, 52, *113,*
    114, 115, *135, 170,* 175, *310,* 313
Dolce & Gabbana, 136
Donovan, Carrie, 6, 26
Donovan, Terence, 126
Doonan, Simon, *174, 175,* 286
Doo.Ri, *198, 310,* 334
Douglas, Meghan, 78, *78*
Downtown-V285, 129
Duffy, Robert, *135,* 239, 261, 294, 344
Duke, Randolph, 85, 89, *89, 90, 134,* 147
Dunst, Kirsten, *313,* 336
Dupre, Ashley, *321*

E

Ebanks, Selita, *357*
Eisen, Mark, 13, 39, 69, 75
Elegies to the Spanish Republic, 36
Elements of Style, 26
Elgort, Arthur, *284*
Elle, 17, 78, 107, 195, 229, 274
Elliott, Missy, *359*
Ellis, Perry, *174, 175,* 293
Elson, Karen, *87,* 261, 344
Employee of the Month, 136
Emporio Armani, 106
Ensslen, Katherine, *230, 230*
Entertainment Tonight, 128

Escada, 23, 155
Essence, 274
Etheridge, Melissa, *163*
Evangelista, Linda, 6, *7, 8,* 16, 17, 45, 65,
    74, 85, 85, 89, 90, 129, 255
Extra, 163
Ezersky, Lauren, *135, 196, 196–197*

F

Farrow, Mia, 136
Fashion File, 196
Fashion for Relief Show, 252, 326, 344, 354
Fashion Inside Out, 262
Fashion Police, 254
Fashion Targets Breast Cancer, 27
Fashion's Night Out, 356
Faturoti, Lola, 147
Fawcett, Farrah, 229, 233
Feith, Tracy, 33
Fendi, 136
Fergie, 63, 118, *264,* 338
Ferguson, Sarah, 239, 344, 354
Ferretti, Alberta, 283, 294, 315
Ferro, Stefano, 261
Fetherston, Erin, 268, 283, 287, 290, 292
Field, Patricia, *135, 322,* 334, 359
Fifth Element, The, 48
Filicia, Thom, 217
Fish, Nian, *188, 188–189*
Flay, Bobby, 254
Fogarty, Katie, 315
FOLIO, 46
Fontana, Isabeli, *127, 180*
Ford, Tom, 356
Fox, Michael J., *14*
Foxman, Ariel, *222,* 222
Franken, Al, 129
French Vogue, 187
Friedrich, Brice, 147
Froio, Etta, 23
Fuentes, Daisy, *64, 64*
Full Frontal Fashion, 117, 254, 255
Fusha, 194

G

Gaelyn, Genevieve, 149
Gallagher, John, 283
Galliano, John, 65
Garcia, Nina, *273,* 313
Gaskins, Eric, 33
Gaultier, Jean Paul, 48, 65, 284, 290
George, 98
George, Jennifer, 33
Gevinson, Tavi, 336
Ghesquiere, Nicolas, 155, *155,* 175
Ghost, 13, *50, 72*
Ghuari, Yasmeen, *22, 30*
Gilbert, Odile, *323*
Gimbel, Evie Goodman, 210
Giuliani, Rudy, 106, 244, 361
Givenchy, 187, 314
Glamour, 107, 135
Glaser, Elizabeth, 210
Goff, Trish, 16, *16–17, 40,* 69, *132*
Gold, Jared, 185
Goldfinger, 334
Goldstein, Lori, *195,* 321
Good Morning America, 128
Goodman, Tonne, 210
Gossip Girl, 222
Gottex swimsuit, 229, 233

Grable, Betty, 186
Graham, Gary, 334
Graham, Heather, 313
Graham, Sandra, 85
Greenfield-Sanders, Timothy, 239
Grès, Madame, *311*
Griffin, Kathy, *163,* 222, 255
Grimes-Viort, Ben, *201*
Groff, Jonathan, 283
Groveman, Michael, 195
G-Star Raw, 313
Gucci, 188
Guerin, Heloise, *305,* 336
Guinness, Daphne, 344, *349*
Guinness, Jasmine, 65
Gunn, Tim, 149, 240, 262, 313
Gurung, Prabal, *324, 343*
Gyllenhaal, Maggie, 214

H

Ha, Christina, 117
Haag, Donna, 147
Hall, Bridget, *102*
Halston, 36, 37, *83, 84,* 85, 89, 106, *140,*
    303, 323, 344
Hamilton, Charles, 313
Hamm, Jon, 342
Hannant, Douglas, 34, *196,* 283, *286, 286*
Happy Tears, 344
Harden, Marcia Gay, 89, 304
Hardison, Bethann, 294, *296, 296*
Hargitay, Mariska, 254
Harlow, Jean, 192
Harlow, Shalom, *21, 28,* 65, 69
Harmon, Angie, 189
Harper's Bazaar, 6, 37, 46, 78, 128, 296, 344
Harris, Neil Patrick, 356
Harry, Debbie, *242, 264*
Hasselbeck, Elisabeth, 321
Hathaway, Anne, *307*
Hayek, Salma, 26
Hearst, Lydia, 252, 283, *287,* 359
Heart Truth Show, *264, 282, 283,* 302
Heatherette, 118, *119,* 129, *185, 185,* 207,
    238, 250, 251, *258,* 261, 275, 283, *288,*
    290, 294, 335, 358, 359
Heatherton, Erin, *276*
Hefner, Hugh, 156
Heisel, Sylvia, 33
Hello Kitty, *185,* 207
Henner, Marilu, 39
Herchcovitch, Alexandre, 322
Herman, Stan, 6, 7, *15, 15,* 175, 344
Hernandez, Lazaro, 199, *272,* 356
Herrera, Carolina, 23, 34, 39, *82,* 96, *110,* 118,
    192, 194, 202, 206, 210, 239, 255
Hewson, Ali, *307*
Hicks, Michelle, *53,* 69
Hilfiger, Tommy, 7, *125, 132, 134,* 135, *205,*
    208, 228, 251, *282, 339,* 344, *346, 346,* 356
Hilton, Nicky, *168,* 251, 271, 322
Hilton, Paris, *168, 185, 185,* 271, *358,* 359
Holstein, Catherine, *327*
Honey, 46
Horyn, Cathy, 271
Hourani, Rad, *306, 306*
How I Met Your Mother, 218
How to Marry a Millionaire, 186
Howard Johnson, 33
Hume, Kirsty, 25, 344
Hutton, Lauren, *312,* 356

I

I-D, 359
Idol, Billy, 251
If You Have to Cry, Go Outside, 322
Imitation of Christ, 163, 185, 185, 195
Incident at Oglala, 229
InStyle, 26, 185, 222
Interview, 354
Irving Plaza, 156
Irwin, Elaine, 54

J

J Crew, 255
Jackman, Hugh, 254
Jackson, Janet, 295
Jackson, Michael, 26
Jacobs, Marc, 32, 65, 72, 89, 95, 97, 98, 113,
    118, 123, 129, 135, 137, 152, 155, 160, 175,
    183, 188, 190, 192, 193, 210, 214, 215, 216,
    226, 229, 239, 245, 250, 251, 261, 270, 271,
    275, 278, 284, 294, 300, 312, 315, 318, 320,
    321, 325, 330, 332, 342, 344, 357
Jacqueline Kennedy: The White House Years,
    160
Jagger, Bianca, 33, 33
Jagger, Mick, 313
Jameson, Jenna, 294
Jay-Z, 245
Jean, Wyclef, 198
Jeter, Derek, 175, 179
Johansson, Scarlett, 271
John, Elton, 75, 75
John, Sean, 145
Johnson, Betsey, 7, 13, 14, 45, 52, 55, 55, 74,
    91, 92, 95, 104, 133, 135, 135, 155, 155, 156,
    156, 175, 185, 196, 239, 294, 295
Johnson, Lulu, 135
Joop, 42, 44

K

Kabukuru, Kiara, 77
Kalinka, 12
Kamali, Norma, 10
Kaner, Joan, 23, 36-37
Karan, Donna, 6, 7, 13, 13, 15, 23, 26, 58, 60,
    64, 64, 65, 70, 107, 115, 135, 137, 147, 164,
    174, 179, 180, 210, 249, 250, 255, 256, 260,
    291, 334, 344
Kardashian, Kim, 294, 295
Karesh, Lance, 33
Kass, Carmen, 122, 163, 182
Kebede, Liya, 126, 137, 356
Keeve, Douglas, 23
Kell on Earth, 322, 323
Kelly, Gene, 336
Kelly, Grace, 254
Kennedy, John F., Jr., 72, 76
Kerr, Miranda, 243
Kerrigan, Daryl, 86, 86, 96, 155
Kerwin, Jessica, 334
Keys, Alicia, 251
Khozzisova, Anastasia, 138
Kidd, Jodie, 66, 96
Kidman, Nicole, 26
Kim, Daul, 285
Kitt, Eartha, 75
Klein, Anne, 13, 185, 283
Klein, Calvin, 6, 7, 13, 15, 26, 33, 33, 34, 44, 49,
    53, 64, 65, 107, 115, 136, 148, 149, 163, 187,

188, 189, 195, 195, 210, 224, 228, 240, 244,
    251, 334, 344, 362
Klein, Steven, 284, 349, 359
Klensch, Elsa, 139, 147
Kloss, Karlie, 356
Klum, Heidi, 134, 239, 273, 313
Knauss, Melania, (see Trump, Melania)
Knight, Jordan, 208
Knight, Michael, 273
Kocheva, Angelika, 303
Kors, Michael, 6, 74, 95, 99, 103, 112, 114, 118,
    137, 144, 147, 174, 182, 199, 210, 228, 250,
    253, 273, 275, 282, 360
Kravitz, Lenny, 356
Krelenstein, Greg, 271
Krizia, 107
Kroes, Douten, 209
Kubatova, Eva Jay, 178
Kuhne, Kai, 239, 261
Kuik, Tiiu, 200
Kutoglu, Atil, 322

L

La Dolce Musto, 129
LaBelle, Patti, 109, 198
LaChapelle, David, 126, 359
Lacroix, Ann-Catherine, 108
Lady Bunny, 313
Lady Gaga, 306, 326
Lagerfeld, Karl, 65, 119, 187, 197, 218,
    259, 261, 261
Lam, Derek, 199, 280, 318
L.A.M.B., 253
Lambert, Adam, 129
Lambert, Eleanor, 6, 7
Lang, Helmut, 115, 115, 125, 144, 147, 268,
    294, 362
Lange, Liz, 169
LaPointe, Sally, 118, 335
Lauper, Cyndi, 79
Lauren, Ralph, 7, 15, 30, 34, 54, 64, 104, 112,
    147, 149, 164, 175, 183, 184, 185, 185, 188,
    223, 237, 238, 245, 253, 259, 270, 294, 295,
    298, 332
Lauren, Ricky, 295
Lazareanu, Irina, 303, 336
Le Fay, Morgane, 248
Leacock, Robert, 23
Leibovitz, Annie, 284
Lepore, Amanda, 135, 251, 261, 271, 283,
    294, 359
Lepore, Nanette, 212, 217, 236, 313
Lepore, Violet, 212
Leto, Jared, 271
Leva, Michael, 13
Lewinsky, Monica, 135
Lezark, Leigh, 271, 307
Licht, Judy, 117, 255
Life & Style, 119
Lil' Kim, 359, 271
Lil' Mama, 294, 295
Lim, Phillip, 242, 271, 275
Lima, Adriana, 114
Lincoln Center, 7, 15, 117, 196, 271, 272, 321,
    333-334, 338, 346, 354, 356, 358
Lindvall, Angela, 83
Living Daylights, The, 126
Lohan, Lindsay, 264
Longoria, Eva, 254
Look, 359
Look, The, 89
Lopez, Jennifer, 26, 265, 356
Louboutin, Christian, 338

Love, Courtney, 336, 357
Luca Luca, 154, 162, 175, 260
Lumley, Joanna, 185
Lundqvist, Alex, 63, 63

M

Machtinger, Amit, 57
Mackie, Bob, 73, 175
Macpherson, Elle, 45
Mad Men, 342
Madame Grés, 36
Mademoiselle, 156
Madonna, 23, 139, 290, 326, 338
Magaschoni, 13, 293
Mahshie, Jeff, 261
Making of Fashion's Night Out, The, 356
Malandrino, Catherine, 233, 239, 261, 265,
    350, 360
Mallis, Fern, 6, 7, 15, 55, 99, 117, 135, 145,
    169, 210, 262, 344, 361, 361
Maltagliata, Miriam, 229
Manhattan on the Rocks, 129
Mara, Max, 187
Marc Anthony, 265
Marchesa, 320, 332
Marie Claire, 17, 107, 128
Marie, Lisa, 195
Marks, Heather, 251
Marnay, Amael, 155
Marnay, Audrey, 104, 155, 182
Marquez, Sheila, 336
Martone, Lorenzo, 325, 325-326, 337
Mason, Claudia, 218, 218
Mastroianni, Joanna, 251
Mathews, Dan, 148, 148, 149
Maury Povich Show, The, 210
Maxim, 254
Mazur, Monet, 195
McCartney, Stella, 82
McCullough, Jack, 199, 272, 356
McDonald, Patrick, 265
McFadden, Mary, 7
McGowan, Rose, 242
McGrath, Mark, 251
McGrath, Pat, 326
McKenzie, Jaunel, 209
McKenzie, Stacey, 68
McLaren, Malcolm, 45
McMenamy, Kristen, 39, 344
McMullan, Patrick, 174, 175
McQueen, Alexander, 64, 65, 117, 135,
    135, 344, 345
McQueen, Joyce, 344
Meisel, Steven, 17, 78, 107, 136, 218, 284
Melgoza, Raul, 272
Mellen, Polly, 89, 255
Mellon, Tamara, 303
Mendel, Gilles, 103
Mendel, J., 103, 217
Menichetti, Roberto, 219
Menkes, Suzy, 6, 96
Metamorphoses, 254
Michael & Hushi, 335
Midler, Bette, 336
Miele, Carlos, 321
Miller, Nicole, 44, 62, 64, 75, 100, 115,
    185, 195, 283
Mills, Kelly, 348
Mills, Noah, 232
Milly, 342
Minghella, Max, 313
Minnelli, Liza, 303
Minogue, Kylie, 338

Mischka, Badgley, *20*, *21*, 65, 85, *85*, 185, 251, *255*, 352
Miss Sixty, 269, *318*, *319*
Mizrahi, Isaac, 7, *23*, *24*, *28*, *31*, *32*, *49*, *62*, *79*, *82*, *84*, 129, 218, 222, 254, 320, *326*, 336, 337
Monroe, Marilyn, 186
Montgomery, Poppy, 251
Moore, Demi, 344, *345*
Moore, Julianne, 356
Morales, Natalie, 283, *287*
Mordanova, Ranya, *324*
Moreau, Tanga, *87*, 344
Moreira, Kelly, *340*
Mortimer, Tinsley, *119*, *261*, *271*, 358
Moss, Kate, 16, *33*, 45, *53*, 55, *55*, *134*
Motherwell, Robert, 36
Muhl, Charlotte Kemp, *339*
Mulder, Karen, *22*
Murenu, Luigi, 136
Murphy, Caroline, *54*, 69
Muse, Arizona, 355
Mustaparta, Hanneli, 356
Musto, Michael, 55, *129*, *129*
My Cousin Vinny, 86
My New BFF, 358
Mýa, 207, *207–209*, *271*
Mystery Train, 86

N

Neiman Marcus, 36
Neuwirth, Bebe, *264*
New York Daily News, 55
New York, 55
New York Times, The, 240, 253, 271, 274, 296, 334, 362
New Yorker, 148
Newhouse, Jonathan, *349*
Nicholas K, *319*
Nicholson, Jack, 229, 233
Nicholson, Jennifer, 229, 233, *246*, *248*
Nicol, Geordon, 271
Nilsson, Lars, *163*, 195
Nolan, Charles, 210
North, Chandra, 66

O

Obama, Barack, 304
Obama, Michelle, 76, 293, 304
Oberson, Gideon, 229
O'Connor, Erin, *88*
Oldham, Todd, 7, *11*, *12*, *22*, 23, *23*, *43*, *54*, 62, 68, 69, *73*, *74*, *75*, *84*, 99, 109, 129, 210, 255, 262, 358
Oliveira, Raica, 157
Olsen, Ashley, 323, 336, *347*, 356
Olsen, Mary-Kate, 323, 336, *347*, 356
Onassis, Jacqueline Kennedy, 160
Ones, Malin, *305*
Ono, Yoko, 337
Oprah Winfrey Show, The, 128, 274
Orpheus Descending, 218
Osbourne, Kelly, 251, *252*
Otis, Carré, 39
Owens, Rick, *173*, 175

P

Padilha, Mauricio, 333–335
Padilha, Roger, 333–335

Page, Dick, *139*
Paltrow, Gwyneth, 115
Panichgul, Thakoon, 219
Pantaeva, Irina, *47*
Paper, 196
Parfitt, Jade, 65, *65*
Park, Hye, *243*
Parker, Sarah Jessica, 76, 117, 175, *197*, *297*, 336, 344
Patner, Josh, 164, 210
Patterson, Sean, 63
Pechekhonova, Colette, *116*
Peltier, Leonard, 229
Penn State, *251*
People, 293
People's Revolution, 322
Perron, Vanessa, 200
Perry, Katy, 118, 129, 338
Pham, Thuy, *233*
Phelps, Nicole, 229
Phillips, Sarah, 13
Pierre-Jean, Marie Claudinette, *198*
Pierrot, 175, *184*, *185*, 210, *211*, *216*
Pinto, Maria, 304
Pita, Orlando, 334
Pivovarova, Sasha, 344
Playboy, 156
Playboy Bunnies, 155
Pollan, Tracy, *14*
Poly, Natasha, *220*, 344
Popluxe, 353, 356, 358, 359
Porizkova, Paulina, 78
Posen, Zac, 56, *177*, *188*, *205*, 227, *228*, 239, 353, 356
Prada, Miuccia, 23, 65, 107, 284, 315, 325
Pratts Price, Candy, 164, 344
Presley, Lisa Marie, 135
Prinsloo, Behati, *263*
Project Runway, 118, 197, 240, 262, 263, 273, 274, 313, 358, 362

Q

Queer Eye for the Straight Guy, 217

R

Rabanne, Paco, 322
Rachel Zoe Project, The, 118
Rag & Bone, 208, *291*
Rains, Traver, *119*, 185, 283, 358, 359
Ramos, Luisel, 283
Ready-to-Wear, 129
Reese, Tracy, 13, 283, 293, *293*, 313
R'el Dade, 335
Reyes, Brian, 253, 321, *343*
Ribeiro, Caroline, *138*
Ribisi, Marissa, 322
Ricci, Christina, *109*
Ricci, Nina, 117
Rich, Denise, 155
Rich, Richie, 118, *119*, 129, 185, 239, *239*, 283, 356, *357*, 358, *358–359*
Richards, Alexandra, 217
Richards, Keith, 229
Richards, Theodora, 217
Richardson, Terry, 356
Richie, Nicole, 252
Rihanna, 118, 338
Ripa, Kelly, *282*
Ritts, Herb, 107
Rizer, Maggie, *97*, *98*, 109
Robert Verdi Show, The, 254

Robinson, Patrick, 102
Rocha, Coco, 284, *284*, 321
Rock & Republic, 268, 283
Rodarte, 266, 270, 300
Rodman, Dennis, 149, 239
Rodriguez, Narciso, 72, 76, *76*, 118, *175*, 216, 234, 270, 312
Rogers, Mimi, 210
Roi, Alice, 229
Roitfeld, Carine, *349*
Roker, Al, 283
Romijn, Rebecca, 83
Ronson, Charlotte, 283, 292
Roslyakova, Vlada, 336
Rossellini, Isabella, 45, *45*, 239
Rossi, Sergio, 164
Roth, David Lee, 39
Rourke, Mickey, 39
Rowley, Cynthia, 45, 62, 64, *104*, 125, *125*, *145*, *150*, *163*
Roy, Rachel, 308
Ruby Slipper Collection, *312*
Rucci, Ralph, 36, *36*, 65, *249*, *258*, 339
RuPaul, *14*
Russell, Cameron, 220
Russo, Anna Dello, 306, 349
Ruttenstein, Kal, *168*
Ruzow, Stephen, *163*
Rykiel, Sonia, 322

S

Sacco, Amy, 135
Sacramone, Alicia, 313
Saint Laurent, Yves, 17, 236
Saint Louis Augustin, Chrystele, *38*
Saltzman, Ellen, 26
Salvail, Ève, *11*, *48*, *48*
Sandberg, Emily, 136, *136*, 137
Santos, Ana Bela, *178*
Sarafpour, Behnaz, *214*, 217, 294
Sarandon, Susan, 79, 345
Sarofim, Allison, 337
Sartorialist, The, 164
Saun, Kara, 33, 240, *240–241*
Saunders, Jennifer, 185
Saunders, Jonathan, 303
"Save the Garment Center," 313
Savile Row, 82
Scaasi, Arnold, 23, 274
Schenkenberg, Marcus, 163
Schiffer, Claudia, 6, 45, 69, 85
Schouler, Proenza, 199, 217, 227, 238, 272, 275, 320, 356
Scott, Jeremy, *184*, 195, 260, 269, 353
Scott, L'Wren, 313
Sean John, 195
Sebelia, Jeffrey, 273
Secretary, 214
Sedgwick, Edie, 156
September 11, 2001, 169, 171, 175, 176, 196
Sevigny, Chloë, *145*, 155, 157, *163*, 323
Sex and the City, 98, 274, 359
Seymour, Stephanie, *144*
Shaffer, Bee, 336
Shakira, 251, 338
Shall We Dance?, 207
She's Got the Look, 254
Shields, Brooke, 210, 345
Shopping Diet, The, 26
Silverstone, Alicia, 185
Simmons, Kimora Lee, 119, *168*, 208, 251, *287*
Simmons, Russell, *14*, 129
Singer, Sally, 118, 307

Siriano, Christian, 313
Sitbon, Martine, 293
Slaviero, Guisi, 46
Slowey, Anne, 229
Slowik, Stephen, 147, 163
Smaldone, Michael, 210
Smith, LaQuan, 348, 348
Smith, Patti, 37, 344
Smith, Willi, 296
Smither, Beri, 33, 107, 107
Snow, Carmel, 37
Snyder, Dean, 56, 56
Som, Peter, 334
Souleiman, Eugene, 175
Spears, Britney, 338
Spelling, Tori, 195, 245
Spitzer, Eliot, 321
Sports Illustrated, 107
Sprouse, Stephen, 96, 96, 175
Stam, Jessica, 227, 256, 327
Stange, Iekeliene, 303
Starring, 195
Stefani, Gwen, 106, 253, 271, 359
Steffe, Cynthia, 194
Stephenson, Mary Alice, 128, 128
Stern, Molly R., 186
Sternberg, Scott, 313
Stewart, Martha, 37
Stokes, Stormy, 244
Stone, Joss, 251
Stone, Lara, 276
Stripes of the Tiger, 23
Strubegger, Iris, 187, 187
Struss, Kasia, 285
Stuart, Jill, 60, 85, 133, 158, 173, 174, 283
Sturm, Yfke, 127
Style Court, 117
StyleNoir, 274
Stylista, 98
Subkoff, Tara, 157, 163, 195, 223, 271, 356
Sui, Anna, 6, 8, 16, 17, 22, 31, 62, 75, 94, 98, 104, 122, 136, 137, 161, 162, 174, 182, 184, 189, 204, 210, 229, 236, 271, 294, 316, 332
Summerford, Farrah, 47
Surprise by Design, 254
Suvari, Mena, 271, 327
Swank, Hilary, 89, 163
Swidrak, Brigitte, 186

T

Tagliapietra, Robert, 231, 313
Talk, 274
Talley, André Leon, 64, 118, 239, 296, 348, 354, 354, 356
Tam, Vivienne, 120, 132
Tansky, Burt, 23
Tavares, Fernanda, 193, 210
Taylor, Ann, 275
Taylor, Niki, 33, 75
Taylor, Rebecca, 223
Teen Vogue, 251
Tennant, Stella, 344, 356
Tezel, Sophia, 33
Thakoon, 219, 343
Thalia, 264
Theallet, Sophie, 56, 313, 344
This Morning, 65
Thomas, Marisol, 163
Thomas, Rob, 163, 251
Thormann, Katrin, 336
Tilberg, Tasha, 67
Tilberis, Liz, 109
Tilbury, Charlotte, 334

Tilly, Jennifer, 85, 85
Timberlake, Justin, 349
Titel, Ohne, 315
Today, 283
Toi, Zang, 13
Toledo, Isabel, 23, 283
Tracy, Ellen, 125
Treacy, Karl, 251
Treacy, Philip, 124
Trentini, Caroline, 251
Tricomi, Edward, 34, 34, 336
Trigère, Pauline, 37
Trump, Donald, 106
Trump, Ivana, 27
Trump, Ivanka, 95
Trump, Melania, 106, 124, 239
Truth or Dare, 23
Tucker, Toby, 185
Tuleh, 137, 210, 215, 216, 302
Turlington, Christy, 7, 8, 13, 13, 16, 129, 255
Turner, Kathleen, 109
Tyler, Richard, 11, 13, 42, 61, 62, 75, 91, 271
Tyler, Steven, 45, 45, 359

U

Uberti, Nikki, 334
Uemura, Shu, 175
Unzipped, 23, 24, 196

V

V, 187
Valentino, 187, 218
Valletta, Amber, 69, 195, 344
Valley, Alvin, 321, 322
Valvo, Carmen Marc, 229, 283
van der Klooster, Sylvia, 116
van der Vliet, Patricia, 335
van Seenus, Guinevere, 57
Vanity Fair, 359
Vass, Joan, 48, 114
Vaughn, Mo, 175
Verdi, Robert, 117, 254, 254–255
Vereen, Ben, 198
Vergara, Sophia, 163
Verrier, Ashleigh, 272
Versace, Donatella, 85, 106, 139
Versace, Gianni, 17, 26, 55, 63, 96, 107, 218, 290, 362

Versus, 75, 85, 106, 134
Veruschka, 135
Village Voice, 129, 240
Vittadini, Adrienne, 22
Vodianova, Natalia, 167, 210, 211, 261, 283
Vogue, 6, 17, 34, 36, 98, 128, 210, 244, 284, 296, 334, 336, 344, 354, 356
Vogue Italia, 17, 98, 136, 296
Vollbracht, Michael, 195, 210
von Furstenberg, Diane, 6, 14, 160, 184, 194, 251, 262, 271, 283, 291, 301, 334, 336, 348
Vosovic, Daniel, 262–263
Vreeland, Diana, 354
Vuitton, Louis, 17

W

W.., 34
Wang, Alexander, 271, 275, 277, 281, 301, 303, 328, 331, 332, 336, 344, 352, 356
Wang, Vera, 34, 139, 269, 270, 303
Warhol, Andy, 96, 354
Warren, Joel, 34
Washington, Rudy, 106
Wasson, Erin, 166, 174, 228, 303
Webb, Veronica, 45
Weber, Bruce, 63, 107
Weinberg, Rebecca, 135
Weinstein, Harvey, 303
Weir, Johnny, 271
Weisel, Heidi, 33
Weisz, Rachel, 76
Wek, Alek, 88, 132
Wells, Linda, 139
Westwood, Vivienne, 124, 229, 322
Where D'Ya Get That?, 117
Whitcomb, Laura, 33
White, Constance, 117, 274, 274, 334
Wiedemann, Elettra, 239
Williams, Ronald A., 229
Williams, Tennessee, 218
Williams, Vanessa, 313
Williamson, Matthew, 193, 226
Wilmot, Paul, 244, 244
Wilson, Patti, 359
Wilson, Rita, 356
Winfrey, Oprah, 304
Winslet, Kate, 76
Wintour, Anna, 14, 17, 27, 64, 117, 119, 129, 135, 175, 179, 271, 275, 307, 327, 336
Witherspoon, Reese, 163
Wizard of Oz, The, 207, 283, 312
Wolf, Brana, 360
Wolkoff, Stephanie Winston, 356
Women's Wear Daily, 64, 147, 274, 334, 362
Wood, Steve, 13
Wu, Jason, 275

Y

Yamamoto, Yohji, 283, 336, 349
Yeager, Lyn, 339
Yeohlee, 23, 229, 362
Yorio, Ty, 176
Y-3, 283, 336

Z

Z Spoke by Zac Posen, 353, 356
Zahm, Olivier, 349
Zanini, Marco, 303
Zelyaeva, Valentina, 223
Zhou, Wen, 242
Zidane, Zinedine, 336
Ziff, Sara, 177
Zoe, Rachel, 303, 345
Zohn, Ethan, 175
Zoolander, 48, 358

PHOTOGRAPHY CREDITS

Runway and front-row photos © Randy Brooke

Backstage and runway photos © Roxanne Lowit

Page 107: Beri Smither, © Susan Bowlus

Page 126: Waris Dirie, © Karl Holzhauser / Waris Dirie Foundation

Page 136: Emily Sandberg, © Dorian Caster

Page 148: Dan Matthews, © Todd Oldham

Page 188: Nian Fish courtesy of David Ajbodji

Page 254: Robert Verdi, © Fadil Berisha

Page 325: Lorenzo Martone, © Felicia Lebow

Page 333: Roger and Mauricio Padilha courtesy of MAO PR

Page 338: The Blonds, © Mike Ruiz

Page 358: Richie Rich courtesy of Sarah Basset and Sandra Blume

Page 361: Fern Mallis, © Timothy Greenfield-Sanders

Popluxe photos, © Sarah Bassett

Back cover jacket photo (top image): AP Photo/Diane Bondareff

Back cover case photo (vertical): AP Photo/Zack Seckler

ACKNOWLEDGMENTS

THIS BOOK HAS BEEN AN ABSOLUTE JOY TO WRITE. THE FOLLOWING PEOPLE MADE IT EVEN MORE SO.

Jack Cesarano, for your patience and incredible support.

Iris Soricelli, for picking up the slack while I worked, as well as for your guidance.

Mike Cesarano, my incredible archivist.

James Aguiar, who transformed this project for me. I don't know that I can fully communicate how grateful I am for your contribution to this book.

The amazing Randy Brooke. You made my job so much easier with your fantastic photos. I am awed by the amount of work you put in, your professionalism, and your dedication.

The legendary Roxanne Lowit. What a privilege it's been working with you. You are an amazing person, and an inspiration.

Kelly Cutrone for your invaluable advice and guidance. You are just the coolest ever.

My wonderful agent Celeste Fine.

My editor Cindy De La Hoz. Thank you so much for loving this book and working as hard as I did.

Deborah Kohan, who made it all a reality.

Bethann Hardison and Naomi Campbell.

Georgina Chapman and Caroline Curtis.

Alan Mell, Berty Elkind, Rae Cesarano, Jill Helene Fettner, Barbara Levy, and Patrick Mitchell, for taking this journey with me.

Amanda Richmond and Chris Navratil from Running Press.

Katherine Ensslen, Gordon Espinet, and Luc Bouchard from MAC.

Eric White and Shoko Takayasu.

André Leon Talley, Glenda Bailey, Candy Pratts Price, and Narciso Rodriguez.

Rosina Rucci, Stacey McKenzie, Allee Newhoff, Alison Levy, Robert Verdi, Megan Soricelli, Suzanne Levinson, Richard Levy, Evan Levy, and Eric Burak.

Felicia Lebow, for my wonderful photo. Your support has meant so much to me.

Finally, Mark A. Lyons. You have been truly incredible. I can't imagine what this process would have been like without you, but I know it wouldn't have been half as much fun. I cannot thank you enough for your generosity, hard work, and support.

RANDY BROOKE would like to thank all the people that make fashion week(s) better, including the photographers who help out—with special thanks given to Tom Concordia.

ROXANNE LOWIT wishes to thank Eric White, Shoko Takayasu, and Krystallynne Gonzalez.